With a Capital O
A Memoir of Teaching in Rural One-Room Schools

By Genieva B. Pawling

This is a work of nonfiction. To maintain the anonymity of the individuals involved, some names, locations, and details have been altered.

Copyright © 2021 Genieva B. Pawling

All rights reserved. No part of this book may be reproduced or used in any manner without the prior written permission of the copyright owner, except for the use of brief quotations in a book review.

Table of Contents

Editorial Note
Introduction
Dedication
Chapter 1   Credentials
Chapter 2   Pure Gold
Chapter 3   Hiring Out
Chapter 4   Gobbler's Knob
Chapter 5   The Twelve
Chapter 6   The First Dollar
Chapter 7   The Curriculum
Chapter 8   Summer School
Chapter 9   Holidays and Vacations
Chapter 10 Second Only to Christmas
Chapter 11 Personalities
Chapter 12 Winners
Chapter 13 Year of the Influenza
Chapter 14 A Place to Stay
Chapter 15 Away From Home
Chapter 16 Behind the Scenes
Chapter 17 Decorum
Chapter 18 Discipline
Chapter 19 Board Again
Chapter 20 Schwingles
Chapter 21 Compulsory Attendance
Chapter 22 Finis/My Marriage
About the Author

Editorial Note:

This book written in approximately 1977. It is important to note that the author received her education before the First World War. Grammar and punctuation conventions have changed in the last century. This book is presented as it was written, save for typographical corrections and minor punctuation changes made for clarity. Some of the grammar and punctuation uses might strike contemporary readers as archaic.

Introduction

The author, my grandmother, was one of thousands of young women who taught in one-room schoolhouses in the early twentieth century. Grandma started teaching in 1916 or 1917 in rural Steuben County in Western New York. She taught at Boyd's Corners and Lyons in Woodhull, Hedgesville (District 8), the Greenville school in Haskinville, and perhaps others. The Gobbler's Knob school in this book is a composite of these schools.

The one-room schoolhouse system began in the mid-nineteenth century. Schoolhouses had to be within walking distance of all children, so there were nearly 400 of them in Steuben County alone. They went up to sixth grade, which was all the education most children got or thought they needed. If they wanted to go beyond that, they had to go to a "big school," as the centralized junior high/high schools were called. This often meant boarding in a neighboring town, as transportation was not available. The one-room school system was already coming to an end by the 1920s as centralized schools were extended to cover the lower grades and the schoolhouses were phased out. The last schoolhouse in Steuben County closed in 1961.

Grandma was born Genieva Bouton in 1898 in the farming village of Parallel, New York on the New York-Pennsylvania border. Her parents sacrificed to send her to high school, although many relatives thought it was a waste of money. She put the investment to good use, going on to a brief teacher's training and right into teaching.

As related in the book, she married Kenneth Pawling (K.P.) on July 1, 1922. She continued teaching while maintaining the home on the farm and raising three children. In fact, my father, her youngest, never had another teacher until he went to the big school for seventh grade. She taught until 1941 or '42. Grandma authored many published poems and short stories. She wrote two other books in addition to this one. Over My Shoulder relates her early life and Echoes of Woodhull is a local history of Woodhull, New York.

My personal memories of Grandma centered around visits to the "house on the hill," where she lived until K.P. died in 1966, and the smell of baking bread, something she continued to do every week into her 80s. Until I read this book, all I knew about her teaching experiences was what my father told me. She instilled in him a love of literature and poetry that he shared with my sisters and me. She lived to be 97 years old, passing away on Jan 15, 1996.

~ Colleen L. Pawling

For Happy

Chapter 1
Credentials

At a high school graduation in the 1910 to 1920 period, the question was sure to be asked about any of the young people on the roster, "What will he or she do with life?" In the case of a girl the next question would be, "Will she make something of herself, or will she get married?"

The answer in my case would have been doubtful as neither prospect seemed glowing. The oldest of a family of eight children, I had a sturdy body and enjoyed muscular activity. My favorite diversions were memorizing poetry and pulling one end of a crosscut saw, with lesser ones in between.

One of my highest aspirations was to win the approval of my cousin John, who seemed to me to be the peak of sophistication. He lived in a small town and like to point out in a fatherly way my homemade clothes, simple pleasures, and countrified ways generally. He would probably have fainted if he had known about my boyfriend, Henry. Henry worked for a farmer for his board and a small allowance, but had been warned to stay away when John was visiting at our house. Fortunately John lived 35 miles away and his visits were not frequent.

In 1915 when I was preparing for a limited career in teaching, the approved method of qualifying for a rural position was to take a one year course in a Teacher's

Training Class. Such a class was being offered in Addison, 12 miles from my home as the crow flies, 16 if one went to Woodhull and took the bus that had recently replaced the horse drawn stage.

Those who were really serious about devoting their lives to teaching -- some men and a very few women -- went to a Normal School now known as Teachers College. Most young women who were qualifying for teaching expected to be promoted to a position of wife and mother after a few years. This was not so much a choice as a prediction. Marriage was the usual and accepted way of life.

I fell into this group, agreeing with my schoolmates that life is not complete without marriage and children. We agreed that marriage meant a home and companionship. The fact that it sometimes meant hardship was beside the point. That, too, was an accepted way of life.

My prospects for marriage were not the best. In high school I had been something less than a belle. I was strictly the country cousin and, while many others came from the country too, I was naturally shy and quiet. I hoped that a career in teaching would improve my image and my eligibility.

This was a hope I kept strictly to myself. I knew that my parents were expecting me to help with the farm mortgage. With all the exuberance of youth I looked forward to clearing up all the family indebtedness and I was eager to begin. I supposed that the mortgage would soon be lifted and I could devote myself to more romantic interests.

Of formal credentials verified by ornate pieces of paper, I am sparsely equipped, and the more imposing ones I earned after I began teaching represent experience as well as scholarship.

In view of the family finances it was the low road for me. A rural renewable certificate would be granted upon passing certain examinations given in Addison. Having gone through high school on a shoestring I was delighted at the prospect of earning a teachers certificate on another. I borrowed the necessary books and was off. As no license would be granted under age 18 I had a year in which to prepare.

If one's background is a form of credential, mine was one of honesty, industry and thrift. Especially thrift. The people I knew made such items as sauerkraut, soap, quilts, maple sugar and articles of clothing. They smoked hams and corned beef.

They regarded newspapers, when they regarded them at all, as a form of entertainment not especially applicable to their everyday lives. The news of the day was usually communicated by word of mouth.

Woodrow Wilson was in the White House and, we believed, had everything well in hand. He was taking care of our problem in Mexico without reaching into our personal circle of acquaintances for recruits, and he was too proud to meddle in someone else's war. Certainly he would keep out of anything so remote as a war on the other side of the Atlantic Ocean.

The news of his marriage to Mrs. Gault was going the rounds that day in January when I began my quest for credentials. I had read and hopefully mastered the contents of borrowed books entitled "Methods of Teaching," "School Management," and "School Law," and reviewed basic subjects with which I already had a fair acquaintance.

The examinations were held during Regents examination week, the week of January 20 which, in my experience usually blasted the countryside with the worst weather winter had to offer.

The January of 1915 came up to expectations. On Monday morning my father took me to Woodhull with a horse and cutter and I bused to Addison only to find that the subjects I wanted to try were scheduled for Tuesday, Wednesday, Thursday -- any day except Monday.

I spent an hour in the training classroom where several of my classmates were being drilled for examinations, having finished the one year course. A demonstration was underway on the method of teaching fractions, and I listened avidly. It is well that I did as this was the only formal education in school teaching I was ever to receive.

At the bus terminal I learned that the bus for Woodhull would leave at 2:00 PM. The weather was furious. An icy wind from the west brought sleet and freezing rain. The only lounging places in Addison that I could have located were the benches in the park in the one labeled "Ladies Room." I headed into the wind comforting myself with the thought that I would board the bus when it came along.

Now and then a bit of road sheltered by rocks or trees gave me a breather as I turned my back on the wind and buried my face in the fur cuffs of my coat for half a minute-- no more. I was aware of the danger of freezing.

Hours passed. I had no way of knowing how many. My face was numb, though I wiped away the ice from time to time with sodden mittens. When I had covered about half the distance I stopped at a farmhouse to warm my hands. It was not nearly time for the bus by the kitchen clock, and I pressed on.

I was nearing Woodhull and the bus was due when a farmer with a set of bob sleighs and a pressed hay rack asked me to ride. I perched gratefully on the edge of the rack. It was colder than walking but gave my leg muscles a rest.

The man proved to be a Mr. Gross, one time friend of my father. His daughter was a student at the Training Class and he assured me that she would be glad to share her room with me for the rest of the week.

By the time we reached Woodhull I was having such a nice visit with Mr. Gross that I elected to ride on to the next road leading toward home thus adding three miles to the distance. This road lead past the schoolhouse on Gobbler's Knob where my mother was teaching at the time. I hoped to reach it in time to ride home in the cutter with a blanket around my chilled legs.

It was a vain hope. She had left. I enjoyed the remaining warmth for a few minutes, but one of those schoolhouses cooled quickly after the wood fires were banked for the night and I soon faced the last two miles.

My parents were wondering. They had expected me to come directly home from Woodhull by the nearest way. As soon as the chores were finished, my father would hitch up and start to meet me. I managed to arrive in time to prevent his doing so. This was fortunate as he would never have gone via Gobbler's Knob.

I was more than glad to open the heavy door of our rambling old farmhouse, soak up heat from the wood burning heater, sit alone at the long table, and eat the stew that my mother had kept hot on the back of the stove for me.

On Tuesday I discovered that the examinations I was taking were identical to those given the Training class students. The week passed swiftly. I stayed with Mr. Gross's daughter and had lunch each day with several students and two teachers, one of whom was entertaining the group with tales of a young man who had substituted for a sick teacher "without so much as a day's professional training!" This served to take the wind out of my sails and I was careful not to mention my own shortcuts. I was further abashed to find that my walk in the cold did not impress my former classmates favorably. One of them said that I ought to have been spanked. I had thought of it as an achievement. Believe me, it was!

I sincerely hoped, however, that John would never hear of it. A year and a half later I exposed myself to three weeks of Summer School. I did not include pedagogical subjects in my schedule but studied geometry, English Literature, Latin and History in preparation for trying examinations for a Life State Certificate. One of the requirements for that was three years of successful teaching experience. In due time I received it. It was none too soon. The next year the state closed those two heaven-sent loopholes.

Chapter 2
Pure Gold

In 1915, the basic choice for a girl was to marry or not marry. Chubby smiling Henry was not marriage material and I had turned to other choices, pitifully few by today's standards – nursing, teaching, domestic service or work on the family farm.

Oh, there were said to be suffragettes who wanted the world served up on a silver platter but our knowledge of them could be summed up in the words of the popular jingle-

"Don't you worry and don't you fret

And don't you marry a suffragette

Or you'll suffer more than you've suffered yet."

True, my father knew a man whose daughter had become a stenographer, aided by a city aunt. I didn't have that kind of an aunt, had never seen a typewriter, and didn't give that occupation a second thought.

The very word <u>nurse</u> terrified me. I was so shy and so healthy that I had never seen a nurse in action. The thought of laying hands on a fellow human, even on an errand of mercy, was unthinkable.

There must have been training available that would have overcome my reluctance but I did not know of it. So far as I was concerned, the situation was pretty well summed up in a conversation I heard between my sister and one of her friends.

Friend:" Let's make ourselves some white dresses and go out nursing."

Sister: "It would take more than a white dress to make a nurse of me!"

I agreed with my sister one hundred percent.

Domestic service I had already sampled. The year I failed Algebra, my parents, temporarily disillusioned about my scholastic ability, hired me out to a family where the mother was ailing. There were three children, the oldest only three years my junior. The job netted much pleasure. The children and I routinely entered and left the upstairs rooms via a ladder, across the woodshed roof and through a window. But there was very little profit and, as a life work, it lacked appeal.

Of course, I could stay at home as some of my classmates were doing and a few of my relatives thought I should. There was no lack of work on the farm. I enjoyed much of it but not as a lifetime adventure.

There remained teaching. That I understood. I loved books and was at ease with children. It was an easy decision.

My parents were in accord. They had known it all along and had tactfully waited for me to come to what they consider to be the only possible conclusion. This was all in the past on that January day when I faced the storm. I began teaching in 1916.

Teaching was not a get-rich-quick occupation. It brought a certain amount of local prestige, called for a hardy constitution, and paid a shade better than dirt farming. As a moonlighting venture for a farmer, farmer's wife or farmer's daughter, it was pure gold. Such a one had no expenses. His living came from the farm and he either walked or drove a horse to and from his school.

It seems that it was a happy time for the student. Fewer demands were made on them, there was less regimentation than today and greater opportunity for individual initiative. Homework was unheard of. If a child took a book home it was because he wanted to, possibly to free him for more interesting uses of school time. There were chores at home that took precedence over scholastic endeavor and any books would be likely to get only a free ride.

The use of play time was determined, more or less, by the children themselves. If they elected to play ball in the rain, they did so. In fact, I played with them. But if the boys laid siege to the girls' "backhouse," something must be done about it. This was outside reasonable limits.

A teacher must be prepared for emergencies, all the way from a broken bone to a broken window. Of these, the window posed the greater problem for her. A child was held partially responsible for his own safety. A parent would be likely to say, "You knew better than to climb out on a dead limb." In the case of the window he was sure to say, "Where was the teacher? Why did she let you play ball in front of a window?"

I found teaching a challenge but I couldn't share the opinion of the teacher I met one morning as I was walking 6 miles to attend a Teachers' Conference. Hers came out something like this: "If I had known then what I know now, I would have committed suicide sooner than teach school."

She was driving a hired horse on a top buggy and I overtook her while she was watering the horse in a peaceful little stream along the way. The horse stood with his fore feet at the edge of the flowing water. She had unfastened the check rein and he nodded his head vigorously a few times to get the kinks out of his neck, then buried his muzzle in the cool ripples.

The girl in the buggy had a round face framed by a wide brimmed hat of light colored straw with artificial flowers. Her suit was a navy blue and stylishly cut.

I was immediately conscious of my homemade polka dot dress and bare head, but there was the problem with getting across the creek without wetting shoes and stockings. I had come "across lots" to this point. If she had not been there I would have taken them off and waded across.

"Would you let me ride across this creek with you?" I asked. She said yes and I refastened the check rein. It was tighter than I would have liked but I could see by the hole in the rein that it was the one to which he was accustomed.

In the short time it took us to cross the Creek and get into the road, we discovered our common lot and destination. She asked me to ride the rest of the way and we became quite confidential leading to the matter of suicide.

It seems she had dreamed of teaching for a year or two and then being swept off her feet into marriage. Time had dragged on to the fifth year and this had not occurred.

I was shocked at her attitude. She had spoken quite seriously and her blue eyes mirrored her disappointment. Although I had anticipated marriage too, up to that moment in my third year of teaching it had not occurred to me that anyone could be less than enchanted with school teaching. I had suffered social setbacks in high school and after, but the school I was teaching had always loomed as a warm haven in a cold world, and Opportunity with a capital O.

My new friend enumerated her grievances: wading snow banks to get to the schoolhouse. I nodded understandingly. I had to do that, too. Building fires in an icy building. I was my own janitor, too. Complaints from parents. I had had a few. The struggle to get home at vacation time. Yes, that could be difficult. And stupid pupils! Well, I had had my share of them but I did not consider them an annoyance. It took so little to please them.

A little consideration and respect does wonders for one accustomed to ridicule or being ignored.

It did occur to me to wonder why she did not go ahead and commit suicide, though belatedly, if she minded the discomforts so much, but I refrained from asking. I didn't want to be left in charge of a horse and buggy not to mention a corpse.

I never saw her again. I didn't see her name in the obits, or the marriage column, or anywhere else.

I suppose my basic reason for walking to Teachers' Conference was my eagerness to liquidate my father's debt. Until I met the unhappy teacher it had not occurred to me that it was remarkable. I also carried my lunch but in this I was not alone. Some of the towns where these conferences were held did not have restaurant facilities.

I reminded myself not to tell John about walking to the conference. I am sure he would have advised me to hire the only auto in the district and pull up to the conference site in a style befitting a teacher.

Chapter 3
Hiring Out

After certification, the next hurdle was to get a contract. Soon after my eighteenth birthday my father hitched the old gray to a buggy and took me to the home of a neighbor who was Trustee of the Gobbler's Knob school district, and I told him that I would like to teach his school. My mother had applied elsewhere to give me the easier post.

Mr. Cranston, the Trustee (I shall always think of his position with a capital T) was a heavy set, impressive man known for his competence. He held offices other than those in church and school, positions beyond my knowledge or understanding. Facing his august presence was somewhat like appearing before the bar of justice.

He lived in a stone house that, to me, resembled a castle. The inside was equally regal with heavy carpeting and walnut furniture. I was awed by the bookshelves – more books than I had ever seen outside of a library.

Mr. Cranston was an elder in our church and, I hoped, thought well of me. I was more than a little perturbed when he did not respond at once to my application but settled himself for an evening's visit, skirting from time to time the subject uppermost in my mind.

The first topic was honey. "Do you keep bees, George?"

"Not really. There's a swarm in the corner of the house. I think the honey is under one of the upstairs chamber floors."

As a matter of fact, it was my bedroom floor that was being so honored. I could hear the bees working there when I was in the room.

Mr. Cranston turned to me. "You're pretty young, but I suppose you have to start somewhere," he said.

My father broke the silence that followed this remark with lengthy comments on the merits of the Cranston team, and I tried to keep from fidgeting.

"You'll probably want to board at home," he said at last turning his attention to me. "I'd want you to get to school early."

"How early?"

"Oh, at least by nine o'clock- in time to ring the bell."

"I'm sure I'd do that," I promised.

"You should."

After a long discussion-it seemed endless to me- about the state of the dairy business, the great man turned his attention to me once more.

"You'll do the janitor work, of course."

Without getting a reply, he addressed my father, "You've got a nice piece of clover in that field south of the road, George. I've noticed as I was driving by." My father praised the season- enough moisture, even temperature.

Mr. Cranston looked at me benignly over the tops of his steel rimmed spectacles.

"While you're there you may as well sweep the floor, you can probably get the children to help you." And again he turned to weightier matters. I was reminded of the time-worn precept, "Little children should be seen and not heard." I waited with what patience I could muster until he spoke again.

"What wages do you think you would be worth?" By this time I was almost ready to bid for the privilege. "What would you say to ten dollars a week?"

"Oh, that would be fine!" I cried. It was twenty-five cents more a week than my mother was currently receiving.

"I taught school for many years," he explained. "I believe that a teacher deserves good pay, and I trust that you will earn every cent of it."

He went on into an account of a young teacher who had tried to draw pay for time when her school was closed for an epidemic which was lawful to do at the time. He had, he said, given her a lecture about starting out in life by trying to get something for nothing. It was, he told her, a bit dishonest. He hoped I would never fall into that error.

After a decent interval of farm topics, the contract was signed and we left.

There were other hiring experiences, one a year for fourteen years. It became the custom as more young people qualified as prospective teachers to come to the school meeting, tying their horses outside and sometimes sitting in their buggies until the meeting closed, to be the first to apply.

There were few men teachers. One or two, known as strict disciplinarians, were in demand if a school got completely out of control.

The hiring out interview offered opportunity for the trustee to bring up any complaints that might have reached his ears. After my initial experience I understood how a trustee could become distressingly candid. I am sure that Mr. Cranston could have done a superb job without becoming rude.

Some common complaints:

The teacher failed to put on the child's rubbers and he came home with wet feet. I and other teachers while trying to be diplomatic made a running mental rebuttal. (The child probably sloshed through every puddle.)

Child can't read. (How well I know, but I'm doing my best.)

Darling got bruised in a fight. (Probably of his own making.)

Teacher shows partiality. (Not I.)

Teacher lacks discipline. (Children who behave at home do so in school.)

Children ate leeks at school and parents couldn't stand their presence for a week thereafter. (More on this later.)

The hiring interview was also the teacher's chance if she was asking to be rehired for a raise or for improvements in the school plant. Being a beginner, I was in no position to ask for anything.

I was delighted with the school plant. It was an enclosure containing a stove, good wood, a blackboard and books. More experienced teachers might ask for more.

Years later a trustee turned down my application, he said, in favor of a woman who had tearfully begged that she needed the money. At that point, in Depression times, I too needed the money. He would have probed my financial status to the core, the more so because my husband had once worked for him and he was curious. I retired from the field rather than submit to his questioning. I didn't feel that poverty was a legitimate credential, but I refrained from saying so.

At a time when the "Powers" were urging hot lunches for rural students, one trustee stipulated that none be served. It happened that his was the only school in which I ever served them.

This was not a revolt. We had a supply of edibles left over from a Christmas party and it seemed reasonable to use them while they lasted. There was an unwritten law among rural people that rules were made to be adapted to circumstances.

One trustee ordered that no child be kept after school. I kept one briefly the first night but circumstances made it acceptable. The subject of discipline came up most often among complaints against a teacher perhaps because it was the easiest to measure. The old pin-drop test had relaxed somewhat but some parents frowned on any irregularity like having a class outside in the shade on a hot day, taking field walks, and other improvisations that became accepted practice in later years.

This was especially true if the teacher was young. The people of the district took a benign interest in training a beginner in the way they thought she should go. Also, a popular teacher could break rules with more impunity than an unpopular one.

This was the general state of rural school teaching when I took the helm on Gobbler's knob.

Privately I determined not to ask my mother's advice for light and trivial reasons. She told me later that she had resolved not to offer advice unless asked.

With that kind of arrangement I began my career and, somehow by the grace of God, survived fourteen years of it. Before those years were finished I had married and exchanged one farm mortgage for another. During those years our home was a gathering place for children living within easy walking distance. It was my belief that in order to bring up one's children, it was necessary to take a hand in bringing up all the children in the neighborhood.

My greatest asset as a teacher was my mother's example. She was an excellent teacher and I had watched her at work. At the very least I knew what a well ordered schoolroom was like.

Gobbler's Knob was fresh from her management and the pupils fell naturally into the kind of order that she had maintained. My other source of strength was a professional magazine to which I subscribed and which I studied religiously.

Chapter 4
Gobbler's Knob

The designation Gobbler's Knob is not exclusive to the wind swept hill where I earned my first dollar. It seemed to be a natural name for high and lonely places. The Appalachian foothills are sprinkled with Gobbler's Knobs.

The interior of the 25' x 40' schoolhouse was not inspiring. Wainscot, walls and ceiling had once been painted a medium gray and, so long as a fair amount of paint persisted, the district fathers saw no reason to repaint. If they had redone it, it would only have meant another coat of gray. Gray was practical. It didn't show dirt easily, washed well, and was receptive to another coat of gray. Besides that, whoever heard of painting the inside of a schoolhouse any other color? Unless maybe brown. One schoolhouse in which I taught was done in blue- dark but not navy.

Gray was fine with me. It was exhilarating enough that I was about to enter the adult world and earn real money teaching real children out of real books. I couldn't have cared less about the color of the paint.

Many of the houses represented there had little better backgrounds. What set them apart from each other was the wealth and variety of calendar art, framed ancestors, Star Soap pictures- 2 1/2' x 1 1/2' highly colored pictures obtained by sending in Star Soap wrappers, bits of tinsel left over from Christmas, valentines and post cards that covered most of the wall space.

If the schoolhouse walls had ever been so adorned,

the energetic women who had received $2.00 apiece to clean it had removed every vestige. The place had been freshly and thoroughly scrubbed as the odor of Fels Naptha soap attested. The blackboard was shiny black, the bookcases immaculate though the paint was worn off around the latches. The flag lay folded on the teacher's otherwise barren desk. The floor of plain rough boards looks almost damp from recent scrubbing. Water pail, wash basin, dipper and soap dish shone on the fresh newspaper that covered the wash bench. A new bar of Larkin soap lay in the soap dish. Fresh blacking gave the huge boxwood stove a dressed up look. In short, the unnatural cleanness was such as to strike awe to teacher and pupils alike.

Reluctantly I dropped my load of pen, ink, ruler, books and alarm clock on the immaculate surface of the desk. The alarm clock belonged to my parents and must be returned each night to do its duty in the morning. It was the only timepiece we had.

The door of the schoolhouse led to a woodshed heavy with the aroma of pine kindling and hard maple body wood- the promise of winter comfort.

In keeping with all this preparation, I was minded to put my best foot forward. I had never been a hundred miles from home, had never seen a merry-go-round and doubted that airplanes were anything more than a glorified toy; but such as I was, I would do my best.

My mother's old book on "Methods of Teaching" had stated that a teacher should be pleasant but firm. So here I was facing twelve pairs of expectant eyes, pleasant, firm- and what else? That was the question uppermost in my mind. It is a difficult pose to hold if you have nothing else in mind.

I entered the children's names in the register of attendance, shuffled and reshuffled the books they had brought from home plus the ones I had brought and finally managed assignments.

As the children busied themselves with their lessons, I penned notes to parents telling what books their children needed, what second hand ones were available, and the absolute minimum they should buy if the children were to operate effectively.

Replies varied. Several asked if the trustee would buy the books. So on another day I pushed my bicycle to the top of the hill where Mr. Cranston lived and put the matter before him. I do not remember who paid for the new books but I do remember the delight with which we opened the package and the sighs of those who turned back to the torn and soiled ones.

Time has a way of filling itself and after that endless first day the hours were not long enough for what I wanted to accomplish.

The students were not a scholarly lot, especially Ellery, the biggest boy. He was a heavy set boy nearing sixteen when he would leave school, taller than I as were several of the others. What set Ellery apart was the blank look in his eyes the most of the time. So few things really interested him.

He was proud of his prowess with the bows and arrows the boys made a little later in the fall. Ellery's arrows carried as far as anyone's, sometimes farther. It was a heady experience to be able to compete with his peers in any area whatever.

He showed me that first morning where he had studied last in the geography book- on page 40, a full double page map of the United States.

I turned back a few pages and gave him an assignment concerning coal mining. When the time came for him to recite, the only answer he was able to give was, "I guess I didn't ever hear about that."

Geographically speaking, his sole accomplishment was to be able to find any given state on the map on page 40. He was equally inept in other subjects. He was conscientious and pored over the pages with apparent concentration. His eyes became red and swollen.

"What are you doing for your eyes, Ellery?" I asked him. "They look red."

His answer, "Ma puts Watkins liniment in them."

I was horrified. I walked home with Ellery after school and suggested to his mother a weak solution of boric acid which my mother used in the babies' eyes. Realizing that there was probably none in the house, I told her that plain water would be preferable to liniment.

The atmosphere in Ellery's home was rather plain. Everything was scrupulously clean but there were no frills. He was an only child and evidently he had not brought home samples of art as other pupils had done. From the set of his mother's jaw I could see that she was not one to welcome advice.

His eyes showed no improvement and I strongly suspected that they were still getting the liniment. After all, I was barely ten years older than Ellery. You can't blame her for discounting my wisdom. His eyes continued to flame but the scholastic loss was not great.

Ellery was a challenge you could break your spirit on but I couldn't do less than my best. Disregarding the accepted routine, I gave out assignments all around and spent an entire afternoon teaching him to do simple short division and, hopefully, to recognize some of the situations to which it could be applied.

He was doing well and was absolutely jubilant. He told me that he "learned awful easy." I closed school in a state of euphoria. The next day I learned one of the sad truths that face a teacher. Ellery had no memory of either the method or use of short division.

"I guess I don't know about that," he told me helplessly. In vain I reminded him of the previous afternoon. He responded with his childlike smile, "That's the trouble with me. I learn awful easy but I forget awful easy, too."

With a Capital O

One of those summers the social life of the neighborhood underwent a change. Dancing had been labeled an invention of the Devil. Some people bemoaned the fact that the music floated in through their open windows. Even with the windows closed it fell on reluctant ears used only to hymns.

The accepted way for young people to entertain themselves at a party was to play kissing games. These varied from ring games with singing such as "Three Old Maids," "London Bridge," and "In and Out the Window," to the rough ones like "Snap 'n Catch 'em" and "Cheat the Lawyer."

The ring games were rather harmless. Couples kissed every time a change was made from the ring to becoming half an arch through which the line of players wound, or from the arch back to the ring. The idea was that kissing thus in the presence of so many witnesses would satisfy one's natural instincts and head off more serious love making.

It happened that a flurry of barn dances invaded the community. Because they were held in the barns of friends and neighbors they were tolerated and became at least semi respectable.

Leon was a veteran of the war where he said he has seen much of French life especially among the girls. How he happened to be at home while the war was still going on, I didn't bother to ask. He was an expert horseman. It was his boast that a girl who came with him had no need for rubbers as he drove so close to house or barn that she could step from the buggy into the entrance dry shod. Very soon Leon became my "steady."

True, John who had a furlough during this time was not impressed but I comforted myself with the thought that my other cousins were not impressed with John. Nobody was impressed with Leon.

Chapter 5
The Twelve

The time has come to introduce the 12 people who attended the Gobblers Knob school. Bernice and Ellery were nearing 16 and would be leaving school at that age. To Ellery it made little difference but Bernice was excited about her coming emancipation and was looking for a beau.

It should've been easy. She was a honey blonde with a flawless complexion and a clear musical voice. She had a way of bringing out some rather unusual statements in her clear penetrating voice. She "did" her teeth, "laundered" her hair, and "cried her heart out" when it was broken by a boy whose name she did not know. Her birthday fell on October 10. On the ninth she packed her books and said farewell, and we saw no more of her except at a party or dance.

Jemima was the shy one, too reserved to play ball or join the other children in games. She wore her dark brown hair into braids pinned around her head in a coronet. So long as Bernice was there she had company. Bernice remained aloof to keep her clothes spotless. After she left Jemima would stand wistfully at the window looking out at the games. As the only big girl she represented the cheering section and was very much on the boys' minds. They all looked for her smile after a good play, and Al was elated when she hid his dinner pail one day while he was playing ball.

I was invited to her home to spend the night. Her father was a widower and Jemima kept a neat house. They played the Edison phonograph with the huge horn painted in the morning glories, for my entertainment, such old favorites as "You're as Welcome as the Flowers in May."

It all turned out well. In the fullness of time, she married Al and they came to our house, my husband's and mine, on their wedding trip.

Ted was tall, lanky and a star on the diamond. He had a friendly way that one favors from his mates and he sometimes wheedled them into doing tasks that he should have done himself.

Orson had a face like a full moon, round and shining. His ruling characteristic was perseverance. Start Orson at anything he could do – copying, doing sums, digging a flower bed – turn your back for any length of time at all, and when you came back you would find him faithfully doing sums, copying or digging. He was such a quiet worker it was easy to forget him and find a pad full of sums or the side yard pulverized. Anything Orson could do, he would do until someone stopped him.

His skills were somewhat limited. When he was up to bat he stood like a little tin soldier with his bat over a shoulder. If the ball came close he ducked. Positively the only way for Orson to score a hit was for the pitcher to hit the bat with the ball before Orson could dodge it. It was one of the handicaps our little ball team took in stride.

By the way, our version of baseball was "three ol' cat." I believe the correct version is "three hole cat." It is a sort of abbreviated baseball with three bases and as few as five players if that is all you have. If you are very short handed "two ol' cat" is possible.

Elmer was an attractive lad with warm brown eyes and a friendly smile, but it was a long way from his mind to his mouth. A question is asked. Up goes Elmer's hand. He has the answer somewhere and, if no one else speaks, it comes to the surface in time, usually correct. Just slow. This didn't interfere with his performance in "three ol' cat."

Cliff's face under a rumpled thatch of brown hair

was perennially smiling. Nothing ever upset him. He was not particularly neat and his teeth needed attention. He had an uncanny sense of numbers but could not read well enough to understand the problems printed in the book. If they were read to him he could solve anything that didn't involve a long computation almost as fast as it was read.

Al was a favorite, nice looking and friendly. His dark eyebrows made a straight line and met above his nose. His mother was widowed and had farmed him out to a man in the district. His employer and wife provided well for him but were firm in their demands on his time. If he was absent from school it was because of the press of farm work.

Among the younger ones, Clarence in first grade seemed the brightest. He did his lessons well and said and did some unusual things.

He brought a geography book to my desk and, pointing to a word in italics, asked,

"Is that English?"

"Yes."

"Can you read it?"

"Yes"

He smiled broadly as one who has discovered an area of mutual interest.

"My mother can read English, too," he said.

He used to come puffing up the hill toward the school house beside me as I propelled my bicycle toward the top. When winter forced a different mode of travel, we were wallowing through the drifts and he was badly out of breath. Mindful of my trustee's admonition I was trying to reach the school house in time to get the fire started and the room at least partially warm before 9 o'clock.

"If I - had - my sled, "Clarence panted, "I'd draw you up – this hill."

The large map hung across the corner of the school room. It was a map of the county and the site of each school house was marked with a flag.

"Here's our school house," Clarence cried excitedly as he studied the map. "I can tell because there's a lot of smoke coming out of the chimney."

In early spring the boys went to the creek to float sticks in the high water, taking off shoes and stockings as a precautionary measure. While Clarence was busy with his bit of wood, a calf came up and started to eat one of his stockings. When he discovered what was happening, Clarence grasped the length that hadn't disappeared and tugged with all his strength.

"I've got to get that stocking," he cried. "My mother will kill me – I wasn't supposed to go barefoot."

With an assist from the older boys he got what was left of the mangled stocking. He never told us how he explained its condition.

Dougie, aged nine, could make more commotion doing less than anyone I have ever seen. He had the laudable desire to write a letter to his aunt. The desks at Gobbler's Knob had tops that hinged at the back and it was necessary to raise the desktop to get at its contents.

After three days of perspiring effort and unnumbered clearings of the desktop to add to the assortment he felt he must have to proceed, it was finished – all three sentences of it.

Reflecting that it had taken all his spare time for three days to write it, he proposed adding a line to that effect but gave it up when it was pointed out that he would then have to add a line to say it had taken four days, and so on into the future.

I have often wondered whether Dougie ever gained enough singleness of purpose to earn a living and if not, how he advanced to much competence. I fear he took a few of the necessary steps under my tutelage.

Each grade had a class in oral reading every day. Oral reading made sense in those days. In many families the evenings were spent reading aloud, the children taking a turn as soon as they could read acceptably. In any case there were opportunities in church or Grange, and a person's education was gauged by his ability to read aloud.

Dougie, a blonde fourth grader, thrust his right foot well ahead of the left when he read aloud and spoke loudly. I can see him yet with his right foot advance declaring,

"Leo the lion was king of the beastards."

Eva was in doubtful health, especially mental, and we were careful not to upset her. The district superintendent who had general oversight of sixty or more schools visited each one once or twice a year. When he came to Gobbler's Knob, Eva virtuously decided to clean out her desk which she kept in a perpetual mess. She began by throwing crumpled papers on the floor. In deference to her condition I merely set the wastepaper basket beside her desk.

Mark, the youngest, was a beginner and made very little splash.

Several of the boys rode bicycles to school and Cliff, who had none, sometimes borrowed mine and they all took a ride. Al would meticulously set his watch with the alarm clock. At one minute of the hour there would be no one in sight. When the bell started ringing the brigade would pedal into the yard and come to a dramatic stop. This would surely have caused some uneasiness if it had happened during the superintendent's visit.

There was an elderly couple living in the district who had no grandchildren to help them. They like to hire Elmer or Al for after school work and morning chores on occasion.

These boys were capable of handling a team and operating a grain drill, drag, hay rake or mowing machine. Plowing was considered too difficult for them, and an adult always rode the binder while boys or women put the bundles in "shocks" or piles made by setting a number of bundles upright, very close together at the top, the bottoms flared for solidarity, and placing one bundle flat on top to shed water in case of rain.

On school days the boys who worked there brought their lunch in a ten pound butter pail that held about a gallon. Among the goodies would be a jar of soft maple sugar. It took the entire lunch period to consume the contents. Everything was so delicious that no boy in his right mind would risk taking anything back. Better to share than to do that.

These were the raw materials with which I labored. I worked hard. The older ones except Ellery passed the Regents examinations and went to larger schools which had high school departments. Two families moved away. The younger children received slips of paper stating what grade they were qualified to enter.

Cliff was taking his father's milk to the cheese factory at Woodhull, and the trustee hired him to take what few pupils remained to the school there. The School on Gobbler's Knob closed its doors and was never to reopen.

Chapter 6
The First Dollar

There is no dollar like your first one. Everything concerning it takes on a rosy aura. This was well in my case as the first payment was slow in coming.

Before a check could be drawn for the teacher it was necessary for the trustee to make up an estimate of the year's expenses, deduct what the state would pay, cause a tax roll to be made out and posted, and for someone to pay his tax.

In actual practice it can be even more complicated. Before a man could pay his school tax he must get sufficient money. He sometimes had to borrow or collect from someone who might, in turn, have to collect. The same $20 bill might change hands several times in rapid succession.

When it reached the teacher it frequently went to pay a bill, perhaps to the man who had to borrow it in the first place. Mine went to feed the mortgage.

I had practically no personal expense. I boarded at home and took a half a hand nights and Saturdays in all the farm activities. My mother continued to make my clothes. One of my teachers had told the derivation of the word "mortgage" which he said meant death grip. I took his word seriously and was willing to toil mightily to loosen its hold on my father's property.

A teacher didn't ask for money except in dire necessity until she knew that the collector had enough on hand to pay. She sometimes drew a quarter of the year's salary when the public money arrived.

The collector's job could be difficult. A standard retort on being asked for money was, "If you get it before I do, let me know."

This was, of course, before the ban on Bible reading in schools. Religious observance was strictly up to the teacher. Some conducted an opening exercise each morning with singing, prayer and Bible reading.

At Gobbler's Knob I took a different approach. The mill wood for use in kindling the morning fire was straight grained pine, easy to split and to whittle. The boys were whittling arrows which they tipped with eight penny nails filed to a point.

While this was going on I sat at my desk reading the Bible and one of the boys suggested that I read aloud. I was hoping they would. Any practice is more warmly welcomed by children if the suggestion comes from one of their number. We were so deep in Revelations trying to predict when the world would end. Like many a wiser one we had to admit defeat.

When arrow making ended we eased into morning worship. In the meantime as a result of Revelations the subject of the Kaiser came up. This was just before the United States declared war on Germany and we were of the opinion that President Wilson would keep us well out of it, a view we held until the actual declaration. The declaration when it came made no great impact on our thinking. I thought of John and soon the news came that he had enlisted.

At Gobbler's Knob we were more interested in that I had inadvertently shot Al in the back with one of the nail tipped arrows. He was wearing heavy winter clothing and the result was not serious. He was gallant about it and did not mention it at home.

One of the people circulated the report that I was "sweet" on Al. Actually I was "sweet" on the whole situation, engrossed in the work and the play. I left home early and stayed late at the school house.

When the weather warmed up, Ellery became sentimentally attached to me. On Saturday or Sunday he would walk the necessary four miles to my home. He was too shy to come inside and played in the barn with my brothers until time to go home. He was so coy in his attentions that I would not have guessed their nature except that he was free in telling others and news travels.

One afternoon he stayed until dusk and was afraid to go home. My brother offered the loan of either a gun or a flashlight. Ellery gratefully accepted the flashlight. He was terrified of the gun. Ever since the declaration of war, one of his greatest worries was that he might have to go.

"I couldn't go," he told us over and over. "I can't see good enough." My brother threw him into a tizzy by saying that he could stop a bullet if he couldn't see it all.

Poor Ellery! Although he escaped the rigors of war, life did not treat him kindly. At one place where he worked he did not live with the family but occupied a back room where his feet became frosted so that he could scarcely walk. At long last he qualified for old age assistance and lived in clover.

It was during this year that the state instituted a program of physical training for rural children, and an instructor was sent from school to school to show the teachers what to do. Many people bitterly opposed having to pay taxes for boys' and girls' exercises. They felt that chores at home and walking to and from school was exercise enough.

The instructor came to Gobbler's Knob and led us in a number of exercises. The day she came everybody got out of some of the afternoon lessons and, as none of us paid taxes, that aspect did not spoil the fun.

There were three young ladies in the district who used to sometimes visit the school. They would be called dropouts now as none had reached the eighth grade. I enjoyed them and looked forward to their visits.

A number of years later when my own children were small I visited one of them in her home. She had a tiny baby and a toddler or two.

It was summer and the baby lay on a pillow in a big chair. Its bottle was laying on the floor and I could see that the milk in it was thick and sour. Flies clustered on the nipple and at the corners of the baby's eyes and mouth. A friend who was with me said as we left, "If that baby lives to grow up it will be a miracle." He lived along with nine others that she raised to maturity.

At a time when circumstances had brought me to a low spot, she was one friend who took the time to write me a letter. She began it, "to my very dear friend." I'm not sure all the words were spelled correctly but she had no trouble at all in making herself understood, and I am glad to call her friend.

It was at Gobbler's Knob that I noticed a phenomenon that seemed to belong to early spring in rural areas. Before the weather permitted housecleaning the mothers became uneasy and attempted to regulate the school. If there were any complaints this was the time when they surfaced.

This particular year, Cliff's father who had a long, drooping mustache like the White Knight in Alice in Wonderland had criticized my work.

I hesitate to confess my naïve counteraction. Believing that it is hard to dislike anyone for whom you were doing a favor I borrowed $.50 of the White Knight. I don't know that it revised his appraisal of my teaching which may have been quite accurate in the first place.

In another school, I was taking farm census as teachers were required to do at that time and found myself far from my room after dark on a winter night. My landlady phoned the people whose census I was taking and asked them to "keep the teacher all night." It was 20° below zero, she said, and the wind was blowing a gale. She might have added that the road I would take was a path through the woods which one could miss in the dark. There was a better road but it would've doubled the distance.

The people where I was had been urging me to remain overnight and after the phone call I consented.

Our little schools may have had serious weaknesses but they produced some sound and decent citizens, people who have been called the backbone of the nation.

It seems that progress has done a few things to almost guarantee juvenile delinquency – kicked out any mention of a Power beyond ourselves, placed barriers of numbers and space between teacher and parent, encouraged mothers to fulfill their own egos leaving children to glean standards where they may, and permitted gadgets like guns beyond the child's judgment to use wisely.

May we hope that today's children will make as solid a spinal column as those who matriculated in schools like Gobbler's Knob.

Chapter 7
A Place To Stay

The question of board was a lively one among teachers in the 1920's. I boarded at home as long as I could, but there came a time when the distance was too great to depend on shank's mare (term for walking) in the winter. In warm weather I rode my bicycle.

When I had to look for a place to stay I learned that I could rent a room with light housekeeping privileges at the Kenyon's who lived near the school I was then teaching.

The room was directly over their living room where heat from their wood burning stove would reduce my heat bills. I had a small, round portable kerosene heater and a very small Kerosene stove with wicks like a lamp for cooking.

Mr. Kenyon owned and operated a hay press which took him away from home several days a week depending on the weather, I went home week ends and saw little of him until the coldest part of the winter. Mrs. Kenyon had been a teacher and would be again when family duties permitted. There were two girls in school and three pre-school children.

When Mr. Kenyon was away Mrs. Kenyon, the girls and I amused ourselves with small impromptu programs. She and the girls sang a variety of songs like "When the Roll Is Called Up Yonder," and "Marching Through Georgia." we recited poems such an "Independence Bell," "The Village Blacksmith," and "Horatius At the Bridge." It promised to be a pleasant winter.

It proved to be a bad year for Mr. Kenyon whose life

as a whole was provident and industrious. The first indication I had of this was one Sunday night when I arrived to a dark house. The Kenyons were out of oil. They borrowed from my small supply enough to fill a lamp and Monday after school, the girls and I walked a mile or two to the hay press and brought back two gallons from the drum that supplied the press. I do not know where Mr. Kenyon was that day. He certainly was not operating the hay press. This happened several times.

It developed that the Kenyons were short of wood as well, though there was plenty in the woodlot. Mr. Kenyon had only to cut and haul it. It was their only source of fuel.

Coming home from school one night I found Mrs. Kenyon on the couch with a headache. The girls were trying to start a fire in the range preparatory to fixing supper. There was practically no wood and what there was was of such poor quality that it had to be practically soaked with kerosene to burn at all.

The girls appealed to me and I was trying to haggle a few chips off the chopping block to add to their pile of half frozen chips when one of the children came running with a warning.

"You'd better run," she panted. "Pa's coming to throw you out of the kitchen."

Mr. Kenyon had always been pleasant when we had met and I wondered how he would broach the subject of throwing me out. The children disappeared and I stood by the cold stove and waited.

Mr. Kenyon came out, rattled the stove lids a little and said, "You don't have very good wood. I'll have to get some in the morning."

Since there would be no supper without wood he went to the barn and brought some pieces of boards, dropped them into the empty woodbox and retired from the kitchen. I also left and the girls continued their preparation for supper.

Little by little the truth emerged. A barrel of hard cider in the cellar was the cause of his downfall. He neglected the hay press, the animals and the family. His disposition worsened when he was drinking.

Mrs. Kenyon and the girls put down hay from the mow for cows, horses, mules and a stallion. They watered cows and teams but the stallion was a terror to them. Because he was always thirsty he was likely to rush to the manger whenever he heard footsteps. It took more courage than they had to lift a pail of water up under his snorting nose.

Mr. Kenyon's father who lived two miles away was the only one to have a calming effect on his son. When things got really bad Mrs. Kenyon would send one of the girls to a neighbor's home to phone for Grandpa. I was told that if Mr. Kenyon discovered that a messenger was being sent, he threatened his wife with a shotgun and chased the courier out of sight lending impetus to her flying feet.

Mrs. Kenyon used some of my rent money to have a telephone installed to facilitate calling Grandpa. Over the weekend Mr. Kenyon kicked it off the wall.

In January because of wood shortage the family moved into the living room and closed off the rest of the house. Mrs. Kenyon cooked over the heater which burned chunks of wood. This meant long hours of cooking for each dish and only one could be cooked at a time.

One Sunday Mr. Kenyon kicked all the loose furniture out into the snow banks. On Monday he brought the pieces back in and worked at repairing the damage. And so the winter went. I never knew what to expect after a weekend.

Since my room was directly above the living room it was impossible for me not to hear what was being said in the room below.

One morning it became evident that Mr. Kenyon, in a fit of temper, had opened the outside door and gone back to bed. It was zero weather and there was no fire. (Unless someone got up in the night and put in wood, it had to be rekindled in the morning.) This was probably not done because of wood shortage. The first words I heard were Mrs. Kenyon's.

"Will you get up and shut the door and start that fire?"

"I told you I won't. If you want it shut, get up and shut it."

"I'll shut It, Daddy."

"You will not. Your mother will shut it if it gets shut."

I went to school. The Kenyon children were tardy but not absent. I never knew who shut the door.

This was before the day of the amateur psychologist and I wasted no time speculating on whether Mr. Kenyon had been potty trained too soon. In perspective it seems that part of the trouble may have been financial. A farm yields very little in winter unless there is a dairy, and the neglected Kenyon cows produced only enough for the table. Farmers for whom he pressed hay may have been in the same boat and unable to pay their press bills.

One night Mr. Kenyon returned from a trip to town with a neighbor, six miles with horse drawn cutter. About midnight I heard him come in -- I couldn't miss It. He was in a jovial mood. The stove door opened, there was the unmistakable clunk of a heavy piece of wood dropped in, the door closed.

"Get up. Jimmy, Esther, Mary and you Mother. See what Daddy has brought for you."

There was a treble chorus of "Candy, oranges!" and a more subdued acknowledgment of sugar, flour, oatmeal and other staples by Mrs. Kenyon.

In mid-February the baby got pneumonia.

The Sunday before Valentine's Day there was high water. The bridge below the schoolhouse was unsafe for travel with water running over the floor. My brother brought me as far as the bridge and helped me get my supplies across. We accomplished this, foot by foot, along the framework of the bridge.

Then he turned back.

I got as far as the schoolhouse without wetting my feet but from there on a small torrent of water was running in each rut. Under the running water was solid ice and the middle of the road was a mass of very rough ice.

I left whatever I could at the schoolhouse, took off shoes and stockings and walked in the icy ruts the rest of the way.

It was not necessary to go through the living room to reach the stairs. I could hear the baby's ragged breathing as soon as I opened the outside door. Otherwise everything was quiet. I went upstairs without disturbing anyone.

The baby recovered.

I heard afterward that one of Mr. Kenyon's mules died from neglect that winter. I had no knowledge of it. Perhaps it happened after I resumed cycling.

The question might arise -- why didn't I report the Kenyons to the proper authorities? Possibly a modern day person would feel it his duty to do so.

To people of that day, and to me particularly, the authorities were to be avoided at all costs. If it occurred to me at all, and I don't remember that it did, I would have known that even Mrs. Kenyon would not have taken it kindly. It would have meant baring family troubles to the world and been a source of humiliation worse than hunger, cold or illness. Poverty is disgrace, no matter how you smooth it over.

Also, the Kenyon problems, taken separately, did not seems so bad to me. We had been out of oil, we had had to borrow as had practically everyone, we had been short of wood at times, and we had had a sick baby. I'm sure we never had all these at once and we certainly had never known a time when the head of the family was in the doldrums.

I considered myself a friend of the Kenyons and, as such, never mentioned their plight to anyone outside the family.

Another spring Mr. Kenyon pulled himself together, got a good job, and the family prospered.

Hopefully they lived happily ever after.

Chapter 8
Summer School

I attended a summer school quite a distance from home. For this I stayed with a relative, a retired lawyer whose son was a dean in a college. It was a six weeks' course but I was three weeks late in enrolling. It did not specialize in educational subjects and I chose basics in science.

Across the street from the lawyer lived the president of the Normal School (now Teachers' College). Between his daughter, Ava, and the dean and his family I was quite thoroughly deflated. They one and all urged me to continue my education along pedagogical lines. The lawyer offered free room and board if I would do so.

My reason for declining was not one I cared to divulge. I was already under contract and my parents were counting on my wages. At the beginning of the urging this was enough.

When Ava became convinced that I was determined to plunge into teaching she gave me leads to far better positions. Again, I gave no reason for holding back. The reasons I had were growing unclear in my own mind.

I knew nothing whatever of the management of the kind of class one finds in a large school system. It became clear as the summer progressed why these people urged further schooling. To them rural schools like Gobblers' Knob were an anachronism with about as much future as a scab on the end of one's nose.

Enough of their viewpoint trickled into my

consciousness to make me confront the question, "Do I really want to spend my life in a non-rural schoolroom?"

I reviewed the pros and cons. I was a country girl. All the things that I loved best -- fields, woods, stars, elbow room, informality, a bit of solitude, even physical work belonged out of town. I didn't really want to cut the cord that connected me with country living.

On the other hand, if I were ever to do so, now was the time. For better or for worse, I chose the country.

I didn't mention the lawyer's offer at home.

My ego got a second blow when I heard the dean's wife say that her husband had politely refused to read and comment on the efforts of a young would-be poet. I had a few home grown verses of my own that I might have showed him. In retrospect I am deeply thankful that I was spared the humiliation.

I wrote voluminous letters to Leon, none that exceeded the weight a stamp would carry. I also wrote to John. John lived far enough away so that it was a treat to see him. In his sophistication, he had shared details of how to keep a boyfriend in check. His instructions went far beyond what my mother had covered. He had stretched my horizons in other ways.

He had foreseen the involvement of the United States in the overseas conflict while I remained unconvinced. No letter came from him but I looked forward to finding one when I returned.

Then I discovered the casualty lists. They were posted daily on a big bulletin board not far from the school and many of the students stopped in front of it as they came from the building. I joined them.

That was the day that the horrors of war became real to me. The first thing I noticed was the silence among the group gathered there. I was amazed at the length of the list. It hadn't struck me before that so many young men were being wounded or killed every day. After that first day I couldn't pass without looking, much as I dreaded it. So many! Could John, wise as he was, keep off the list?

No, he couldn't. One afternoon his name was there. I was stunned. No more letters? No more engrossing disclosures? No more John? My face must have showed my concern, for a young woman who stood near me came to my side and said gently,

"They list the wounded, too, you know. Maybe your soldier is only wounded."

John's mother wrote that a burst of shrapnel had hit him in the head and that he was in a military hospital in France.

I could have comforted myself that Aunt Erma was inclined to overreact. Hadn't she fainted when at age five John and I had run away pulling a toy wagon loaded with crab apples which we hoped to sell for enough to buy a bag of candy?

But this was for real and I feared for him greatly, and for life without him. So much about life and death he might already know and be unable to give me so much as a hint. I thought of his tall figure, his confident bearing and his slender aristocratic face. "A burst of shrapnel in the head!" If by some miracle he were to survive he would be no more than a caricature of his old self.

But life went on for me. The end of summer school came finding me without funds. A letter from home said that they, too, were broke but as soon as the milk check arrived they would send me enough to get me home.

We had other relatives nearer home. The dean bought me a ticket and saw me aboard the train. After a few days with the second relatives, I borrowed enough to take me to Rathbone about five miles from home, sent a card telling them what day I would come and took the proper train. I had chosen Rathbone as the nearest to home and within walking distance.

I walked into a family turmoil. My father had met the

bus at Woodhull, my brother had met the train in Addison and Leon had met the train at Cameron Mills and had not reported back. My mother, who did not trust Leon and, apparently, did not trust me either, feared we had eloped, and had called the law.

It was a week until school opened.

Chapter 9
Holidays and Vacations

Special days loomed large in the lives of the pupils in rural schools. Their lives were more or less uneventful with chores at home and lessons at school and very little else. This guaranteed their pleasure in a holiday even it meant no more than a program and getting out of school a few minutes earlier than usual.

There were six red letter occasions in the school year, barring epidemics. The first one was in no sense a holiday, nor was it confined to one day. It was the potato digging vacation and it occurred only in potato country where the spud was raised for profit. It lasted from two to four weeks. In other areas these days were taken during inclement weather.

Besides being out of school, the charm of potato digging vacation was money. Children who helped at home without pay shared the prosperity with, perhaps, new shoes or winter clothes to tell about when school reopened. They understood the financial facts of life and took great pride in the size of the crop, the prevailing prices, and the number of bushels each could pick up in a day. Anyone who could be spared picked up for a neighbor for 2 to 5 cents per bushel.

My first year in potato country, I was too far from home to go back for so short a time so I shared in this venture. I hired myself out to a man whose wife was ailing. I was to do housework and pick up potatoes in my spare time. His sister-in-law came and took over the housework and I put in full time in the field.

It looked deceptively easy. There were the crates spaced as they would be needed and there were the potatoes, hand dug with a potato hook lying in neat little piles. To put the potatoes in the crates seemed easy enough and I began doing so.

Before the first crate was filled my employer came by.

"Did you ever pick up potatoes before?" he inquired suspiciously.

"Only enough for dinner."

"I thought so. You'll never get anywhere that way. This is the way you pick up potatoes."

He filled a crate almost while he was speaking, scooping up a dozen or more potatoes in his big hands, dropping them in the crate and, almost before they landed, scooping again. One hundred bushels a day was the goal and it was a proud day for me when I reached it.

It was also a very lame and weary day. I discovered muscles I hadn't known existed. To sit on a chair was painful, to rise from one even more so. Getting in and out of bed was an ordeal.

An ulcerated tooth compounded my misery. The fact that a number of my pupils reached the one hundred bushel goal every day helped not at all.

I took a day off and walked several miles to a dentist, sinking into his chair with relief. I had never been hurt by a dentist and didn't envision correctly what the next hour would be like.

The next occasion in point of time was Hallowe'en. Enthusiasm for this observance varied from year to year. Sometimes the local Grange had a masquerade, sometimes there were only pranks to mark the night. On popular demand, the teacher arranged some kind of festivity.

To anything going on at the schoolhouse the invitation was general, but the one I recall most vividly was attended only by young people including my pupils. We prepared bean soup, simmering it on the old round wood burning stove all day. The game most enjoyed was "Drop the Handkerchief," which proves that a good time depends on the company not on fixin's.

On the heels of Hallowe'en came Thanksgiving, basically a family observance but we often had a program at school and historical emphasis in classes. There would be art work, poems, reports and maybe a tepee set up in the yard. This would be made of poles cut and trimmed by the older boys, set up and wrapped with a blanket loaned by some parent. Decorations would be pinned to the blanket. It sharpened the study of the first Thanksgiving.

Of course the Indians had feathers in their hair or fastened on with a head band. Sometimes the boys made bows and arrows.

One year as Thanksgiving approached the children were playing settlers and Indians. One day Dorothy who had a vivid imagination and a colorful personality rushed into the school room screaming, "The Indians are coming!"

The effect was too valuable to waste. I wrote a little play around it and invited parents for an afternoon program. On the day of the program I wanted a last rehearsal. It was too much. Dorothy announced, "I'm tired of this game," and her performance fell flat.

The high spot of the year was, of course, Christmas. I was careful to have each child included in the program and there were times when this took a lot of doing. It was sometimes necessary to write a play around a difficult character, or add a walk-on part to a published play. I never asked a child to recite a "piece" that he did not like. I read poems and dialogues and, one by one, they found something they liked.

One lad chose a poem beginning, "Benjamin Jones was chilled to his bones" --and I never did get him to say it any way except, "Benjamin Jone was chilled to his bone-- "

In one school it was the custom to combine church

and school observance since the two buildings sat facing each other across the highway and included generally the same children.

Parents helped with the preparations and sometimes took parts but this could lead to a sticky situation as I learned to my chagrin. The teacher was always in charge, that is, until --

I had made quite elaborate plans. Two of the deacons played Jeremiah and Isaiah. Three young men in borrowed piano spreads would sing, "We Three Kings of Orient Are." One of the young men was from the Sunday school and was an excellent singer. The other two could not sing and had no church credentials. And I was assisted by one of the wrong mothers. She could sing and would do so if someone could be found to sing with her. She didn't want to perform solo because of her nonchurch status. I don't remember who played the part of Mary but she must have been religiously acceptable as no objection was raised to her taking the part.

About this time the sky fell. I was summoned to the manse for a conference. The minister strenuously objected to the two wise men and the helpful mother.

Up to that time I had naively assumed that getting sinners inside the church was the prime object of the organization. I told him so. He countered that he and others would be happy to see these people sitting quietly in the pews (preferably the back ones?) but not on the platform in the role of entertainers, even though bearing gifts to the Child or singing His praises.

I offered to drop the whole thing. He conceded that since parts had been practiced, it must be tolerated this time but never again. His wife offered to sing with the recreant mother and I left much chastened.

To do the man justice, he was needled into this action by some of the pillars of the church, to quote him "the ones who pay the bills."

The program was well attended perhaps the more so

because of the disagreement.

I heard no more about it until just after Thanksgiving the following year when the minister read from the pulpit the names of those who would be responsible for the Christmas program. He read twelve names, the last one mine. I was ready to drop the whole thing in the laps of the eleven but, one by one, they came to me to say in effect.

"If there's anything you want me to do to help with the Christmas program just let me know."

No sinners were involved on the stage that year though several helped behind the scenes.

Another time, a different situation. In this community it was customary for three schools to combine in putting on the Christmas program. This was a pleasure. Each teacher took full responsibility for her share of the program. One meeting assured us that none were planning the same items. My own contribution need be only one third as long as though I was doing it all. It assured a good crowd.

Some of those programs were quite elaborate. One of the teachers had musical talent; another arranged a little play.

It was a happy occasion.

Arbor Day came in late spring. Its object was to clean the school yard, rake the dead grass if any remained after months of active play, to have a nature program and to set out flowers and trees. The trees usually died, the result of too much strenuous play, so there was always a place to set one.

This brings us to the Last Day of School which deserved the capitals. It usually meant a big picnic. Planning the menu called for diplomacy. Pupils were frank in their suggestions.

"Don't ask Mrs. L-- for cake. She greases her pans with lard."

"Mrs. G--- will bring just enough Jell-o for herself."

"Mrs. H --- brings two whole loaves of sandwiches."

"Ma makes good ice cream --" and so on but, because it is the Last Day, there is no venom in the remarks.

Mellowed by food and drink, people who had had disagreements during the year got together and made friendly advances. If the gripes were against the teacher they made their farewells, for the summer or forever, and could usually find some words of praise. Sometimes as many as eighty people attended a Last Day picnic.

The day usually passed without incident -- usually. One Last Day in the heat of a baseball game, the batter let the bat fly from his hand and the unguided missile hit a small girl in the eye. Her mother wrung her hands and cried, "Oh, you can't see, can you? You can't see," in spite of the little girl's assurances that she could see. Other mothers were quick to wet cloths in a nearby stream and place them on the eye that presently swelled to the size of a goose egg.

The picnic broke up. Fortunately the eye suffered no permanent damage.

These rounded out the scheduled holidays of the school year, and everyone went home to patterns as varied as the children themselves.

Chapter 10
Second Only To Christmas

In the days of the district school a boy could depend on at least one blizzard when the little kids were kept at home because their short legs were not able to walk through the ever shifting drifts of snow.

Big boys, on the other hand, were more or less in the way in the dark living rooms and steamy kitchens. Unless there were definite tasks for them to do they were encouraged to go to school.

One of them was likely to have the position of janitor unless the teacher held it, and many of them did not. As such it was the janitor's duty to get the schoolroom warmed up for the day.

He might be pulling one end of a crosscut saw in the wood yard at home when the teacher went wallowing past.

He would drop the saw, unreproved by his father who was holding the other end, grab his well packed dinner pail, pull the ear flaps down over his ears and "cut across lots" to the schoolhouse.

Once there he flung open the door and a window or two to let in fresh air which he believed warmed faster than stale air, threw an armful of kindling (pine or other quick burning wood) into the big boxwood stove, tossed in a cupful of kerosene and applied a lighted wooden match.

He would listen a minute to the satisfying roar that emanated from the stove squatted in the center of the room with a long length of stovepipe extending back to the chimney at the back wall, sweep out the loose snow and close doors and windows.

By the time the teacher and the other students came stumbling in, the space within three feet of the reddening stove was unbearably hot, the dampers had been closed, and a waist high pile of chunks, some seasoned for fast burning, others green for holding the fire and for deep, steady heat, was piled in a convenient spot. The janitor was ready to brush off each newcomer with the broom and welcome him to the circle of heat.

At the specified hour the teacher delegated one of the boys to ring the handbell. He made sure to ring it vigorously outside the door for the benefit of any stragglers who might hear its clang as it was blown away on the gale, and make haste to reach the door.

After that formality, each one drew up a chunk of wood from the pile and seated himself as near the stove as the heat would permit. Everyone held a textbook, pad and pencil to which he gave attention between surreptitious glances and muffled giggles. It was a free day. Questions were asked without the upraised hand.

The teacher, freed from attention to lower grades, gave herself wholly to the lessons throwing in anecdotes and pleasantries to illuminate the topic. Shy pupils blossomed forth in the relaxed atmosphere to ask questions with which he had hitherto wrestled in silence.

The smallest occurrence took on an added glow of excitement and became a shared experience, the butt of youthful wit and wisdom.

Anything could happen. A pair of sodden mittens could send up a cloud of foul smelling steam so there would be held noses, grimaces, and the distraction of relocating the mittens. The teacher who shared the circle of warmth could conceivably burn her toe necessitating a hasty removal of her shoe to the delight of the boys. A spark might fly out of the semi-open hearth causing a muffled scream from a girl in whose direction it expired. The corner of a book might scorch and smell but, with all their thrill seeking, these young men and women came from thrifty stock and would never knowingly damage a book, or anything else that had monetary value.

Recess time came surprisingly fast. The boys, dressed as for an Arctic expedition, gathered outside the window -- the same window behind which the girls were standing, of course. They wrestled, wallowed, snowballed, and washed each other's faces in the snow making loud outcries of "That's not fair," and "You can't do that to me," encouraged by frowns, shrieks and shouted admonitions of the girls.

If the teacher thought the boys were getting too rough she, or he, had only to make a little magic that would bring the girls in a circle around the desk. When the girls left, all fights ceased and the belligerents came inside bringing much snow and cold with them.

One of the girls was bound to say,

"Do you have to bring all outdoors in with you?" or

"Shut that door. Were you brought up in a barn?"

Lunches were eaten in pleasant companionship with no small fry to call out, "John loves Grace," or write M.L. plus H.S. on the blackboard.

It was not that anyone disliked little kids. On the contrary, they were excellent material for showing off brawn, prowess, or protective virtues. The heady novelty of being without them in the presence of girls spelled pure bliss. The magic worked on the girls, too, and they secretly prayed for a continuation of the blizzard while they bemoaned the cold and snow proclaiming, "You can't do anything in this awful weather."

The day wore away after the manner of days, and the hour came to close the schoolhouse. The boys, mindful that there might not be another such day in a long time, helped the girls around the deeper drifts and through the lesser ones, walking ahead to break a path that would blow full almost as soon as they had passed.

Once home, the boys were more than likely to be asked to help get out the team and sleighs and open the road which, if the wind were to die down, would guarantee a full attendance in school next day. As they plowed and shoveled, a general prayer went up that the wind would refuse to die down.

Chapter 11
Personalities

There's one in every school -- a helpful Hetty, usually a girl -- so charmingly indispensable on opening day and a pain in the neck by the end of the week.

"Miss B ---, Clara wrote only half a page. She won't get a good mark, will she?"

"I wrote three pages. I'll get a better mark, won't I?"

"Miss B ---, Bessie isn't studying."

"Miss B ---, the boys didn't hear the bell. I mean they aren't going to come." And so on to the point of distraction.

She was usually a good student. Her failing was trying to bring everyone else to her standard. The girl who was most troublesome in this regard was an attractive girl with naturally wavy chestnut brown hair, quite charming when she wasn't being over helpful.

Raymond was typical of those who disobey and tell a whopper to cover up. He had been forbidden by his aunt with whom he lived to go down over the bank to play on the grounds that he would be likely to tear his clothes.

It was customary for school children, so long as they behaved, to go anywhere they pleased so long as they were not tardy in returning. These were farming neighborhoods and they were farmers' children. They knew perfectly well what was "off limits" and what must be handled with care.

So Raymond was left all alone on the playground listening to the shouts of laughter that drifted up from the bank. The bank was overgrown with brush and saplings, an ideal place to play Tag, Follow the Leader, or Prisoners' Base. Presently Raymond went down and promptly tore his pants.

He told his aunt that the boy who sat behind him had driven a nail up through his seat and he had torn his pants on it. That story was too thin for even a credulous aunt. She said,

"We'll go right over to the schoolhouse and see if there is a nail driven through your seat."

"Oh, he pulled it out," Raymond explained.

"The hole will still be there."

Raymond admitted that there wasn't any hole and they did not come to the schoolhouse. Again, Raymond had the playground to himself for a few days that must have seemed like weeks until the bank lost its charm and everyone returned to his level.

When that happened Raymond was delighted, His shock of dark hair so neatly combed when he arrived at school became a tousled mop and a broad smile bisected his face.

Once in his eagerness to get into the swimmin' hole he jumped in fully clothed. He said at home that the big boys had thrown him in. Unfortunately for Raymond an adult witness refuted the story.

Ellery was by no means the only under achiever to come under my instruction. Cassie came for a preview a month or two before her seventh birthday when she would be required by law to attend regularly. She was not toilet trained and came reluctantly at the end of her sister's arm.

She clung to her sister until recess when she sensed the informality and went running around the room brandishing a ruler. The bell for order, of course, meant nothing to her. She continued to run and brandish and shout until her sister, her brother and I ran her into a corner, put on her outdoor garments and terminated the visit explaining as we did so the rudiments of school behavior. She left as she came, reluctantly pulled along by her sister.

We all looked forward uneasily to Cassie's birthday but it wasn't so bad as we feared. Her parents and siblings had impressed a few of the more basic rules on her mind. She knew that one stayed at one's seat after the bell rang and returned to it as home base whenever one heard it ringing.

On her first regular day I gave her a sheet of paper and a pencil. On the paper were the figures 1 and 2 made very large. I hoped that she would attempt to copy them. She broke the pencil in two, shredded the paper and scattered all on the floor,

When she needed to go to the outhouse, her sister led her out looking chastened.

For the next few weeks Cassie's yellow head was most often seen bending over the sand box. She had fair skin and would have been rather attractive except that she dropped her head if she knew someone was looking at her. It was a week or more before I saw her clear hazel eyes.

The simplest skills were beyond her ability -- like putting a stick of wood on the fire. She dropped it and broke off a piece of the stove door.

It was her dream to be a school teacher proving that desire does not guarantee aptitude. As a first step she washed the blackboard -- a sloppy job that had to be redone when she wasn't looking. To reach the upper part she climbed on a small wooden box, getting down and moving the box as needed. When she reached the end she looked down in dismay.

"How me get down?" she asked as she fell.

Her first triumph was to place block on block in the sand box to make a castle as she had seen others do. At home, every effort no matter how futile brought a chorus of,

"That's good, Cassie!"

At first she expected praise whenever she succeeded in placing one block atop another. The other children were cooperative. Whoever was near smiled in quiet approbation and went on to other things. With this she learned to be content.

There were others but Cassie topped them all. I found that these disadvantaged ones served a useful purpose. They brought out kindness and consideration in other children.

One example, Clark, a boy of fifteen with a rugged face and tall angular figure, was allowed to "leave off head" in the oral spelling class for which a small prize was offered.

It happened this way -- each day whoever stayed at the head of the class "left off," went to the foot and received a credit. Whoever had most credits at month's end could choose from a box of inexpensive items.

On the first school day of February, members of the class became aware that Clark was at the head. Different ones asked permission to help him learn the day's words. Of course, it was a losing battle so whenever he missed a word each one in turn missed it. Purposely, of course. I knew they could spell those words but I was as eager as they to have Clark win, just once. He did and was so pleased and proud! I doubt that he had any idea of the effort that went into his victory. Certainly no one hinted.

Fred worked hard at being bad. He liked to be noticed and being bad was the easiest way. His sister rode herd on him and reported to his parents faithfully. One parental directive was that Fred should not go to the playground unless I was there also. Since I was as fond of playtime as anyone, I was not aware of this rule for some time.

Fred had a big mouth which he could twist into a variety of shapes and he was a firm believer in getting even. Lacking both size and courage to fight he got even by making horrible grimaces at his opponent when his back was turned. He would give his head a quick jerk, make his grimace and end with an ingratiating smile in my direction all in an instant. With his self-respect thus restored he was ready to go back to his lessons.

He liked to accuse someone of stealing his pencil. For

this he tossed the pencil under the other desk and said, "See, there it is -- right under his desk."

The fact that it was still rolling escaped his notice until it was pointed out to him. Understandably he was frequently in my company.

James, the biggest boy and the most scholarly in that school, was allergic to fiction and to Fred. He would begin a book in good spirits but at the first credibility gap was audibly disillusioned.

"It's all a danged lie," he would exclaim and read no farther unless required to do so.

James was always on the side of law and order especially where Fred was concerned. He might break off in the middle of an anecdote (we mustn't accuse him of telling a story) and say in an accusing tone, "Fred!"

Fred held him in healthy respect and immediately abandoned whatever he was doing or intended to do. James seemed to have an uncanny foreknowledge of what Fred was about to do.

A first grader came to my desk with a complaint, "Bert has my scissors and he won't give them back."
"Have you asked him for them?"
"No."
"Then how do you know he won't give them back?"
"Because I know him."

His appraisal of Bert was quite correct; Bert was that kind of a boy,

It was the endless variety of the job that made it fascinating. It was even more so if, as happened to me a number of times, teacher knew parents, grandparents, even great grandparents. I knew so well why Eldred fumed at injustice, why Isabel was a trouble maker, why Isaac was a bookworm. I knew that this one would be for order and that one would ever tempt Providence to learn whether rules could be broken. One was curious beyond the printed word while another studied with an eye on what he thought the teacher would ask.

That kind of background knowledge made the job easier and I missed it when I went into unfamiliar territory.

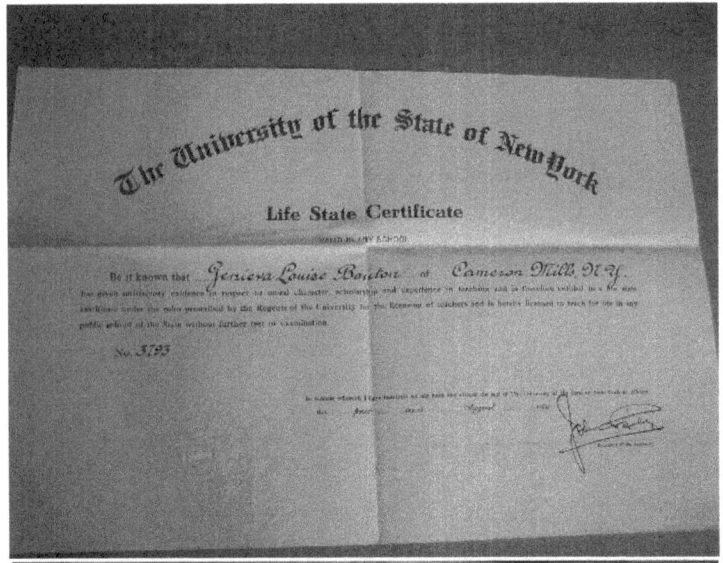

teacher would ask.

That kind of background knowledge made the job easier and I missed it when I went into unfamiliar territory.

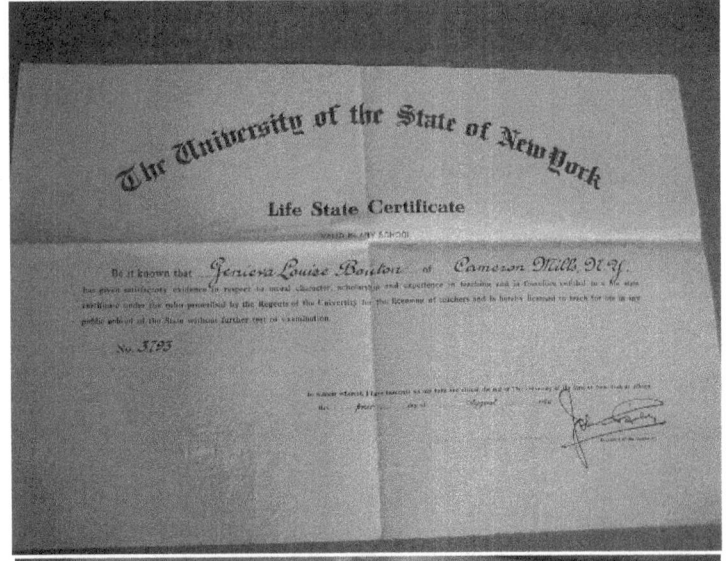

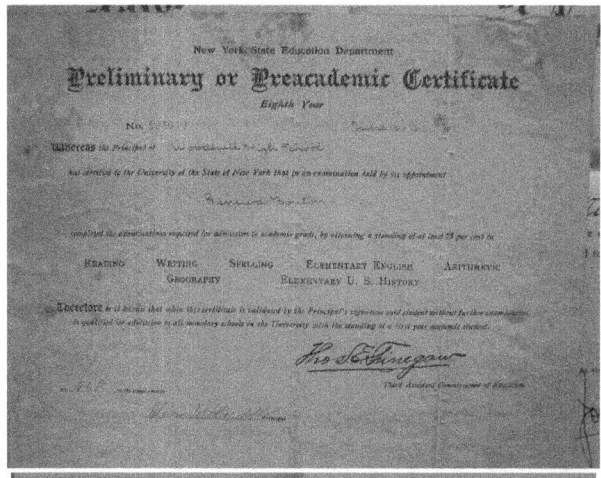

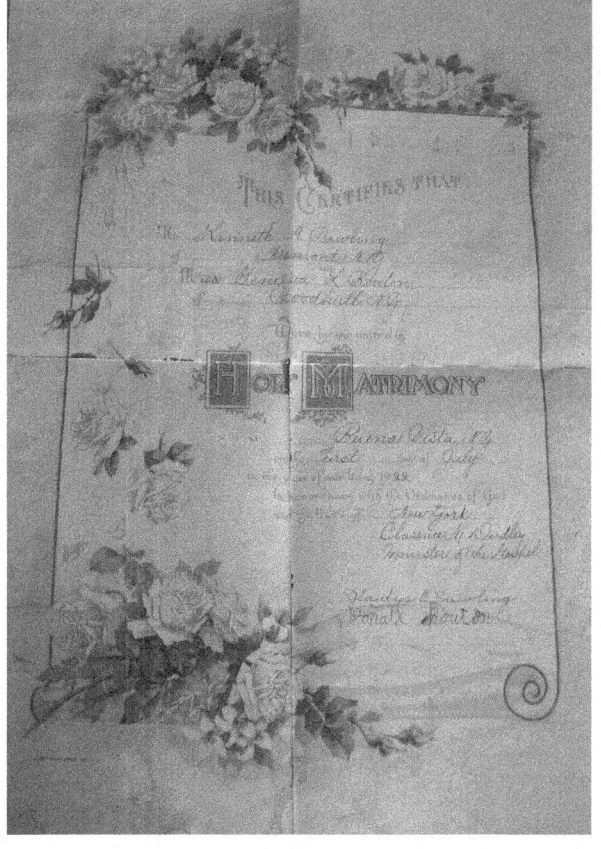

Pawling Family- (back) K.P. and Genieva (front) William, Happy, and Shirley

Bouton Family – (back) Genieva, Grace, George (front) Don and James

Chapter 12
The Winners

So far, this account seems to lean toward the negative. Not to leave a false impression, I will introduce some of the better students -- the ones who make a teacher proud.

First, Polly. She entered school in the fall having attended elsewhere the preceding year until winter weather became too severe for a little girl to walk the distance.

There were no plowed roads unless the farmers themselves plowed them which he would do in an emergency. Otherwise he was likely to say, "Nature put it there, Nature will take it away."

Polly entered first grade with four others, two of them with their thumbs in their mouths, one sucking two fingers and one with half a grimy fist in his maw. From the first it appeared that she was much more competent than the four. She was a year older and school was not strange to her.

I gave her her head as they used to say of a horse driven with a loose rein, and how she forged ahead! It was a day of workbooks. I gave her one and she settled down and did it -- nonstop. One after another she zipped through the material.

The family moved at Hallowe'en time and Polly went to a large consolidated school. I sent a note recommending that she enter second grade which she did and passed with flying colors. A prodigy? No, only more mature than the average beginner. After that spurt she settled down to a grade a year.

Some of the special ones were so not because of scholastic ability but for kindness, maturity or integrity. Such a one was Dorothea. She was fourteen when I knew her. I do not remember her grade or marks. She was small for her age, thin and seriously asthmatic. I remember her for her good nature, unselfishness and courage.

She never complained even when every breath was a gasp. One afternoon in zero weather several of us were shivering as we loitered along a country road waiting for Dorothea who was having an attack of asthma. The sweat was pouring from her face and she was struggling for breath. On other days her sunny disposition lightened every group and was a deterrent to squabbles and sharp words. At fourteen she was a success as a human being than which there is no greater.

Children usually agree in welcoming a vacation. Not so Mitchell. He stubbornly insisted that he could take it or leave it and would as soon leave it. This was in keeping with his character. He made no effort to conform and was frequently on the opposite side from everyone else. He had a poker face and when he made a statement on some unusual subject it was impossible to tell whether he was stating a fact or indulging in a flight of fancy.

He once described in detail a complicated process for getting metal out of ore. I had never heard of it but I knew Mitch too well to argue. A few minutes later I asked him to repeat it for one of the class. He screwed his features into an expression of distress and said, "Oh, I just made that up."

"It might work, though," he added.

When one of his ideas sounded so preposterous that no one believed it, he was likely to dig in his pocket and produce proof.

He had trouble keeping his desk in order. He collected nails, pieces of metal, clippings, pamphlets and what-not which he stored in his desk until it overflowed and the treasures began falling out. Then he stacked his books in the seat beside him to make room for the junk until there was scarcely room for him. About once a week when this happened, he would eye the stack with an aggrieved expression, have a general housecleaning and announce, "This is the way I'm keeping my desk from now on."

You can't fault him entirely for his squirrel like tendencies. When the door knob mechanism broke, he dug into his miscellany and promptly fixed it.

He did everything as though he had all the time in the world yet he was seldom tardy. He lagged behind the other children when going home from school. One night to the surprise of all he strode forward at a brisk pace, put himself in the lead and declared, "This is my usual gait."

He told the most outrageous tales of his own prowess. To explain why he no longer carried a knife he said that while throwing his knife at a target, he missed, severed the belt on his mother's sewing machine and killed his father's best cat. I once believed that nothing Mitchell could do would surprise me, but it did; the last I heard he was preaching.

Jack was a born executive. If he reached the school house ahead of me in the morning there was always a nice fire when I got there, but if there was any other child present – down to and including a first grader – that child had done the work. If Jack was the only one he would do it.

The school could safely be left in his charge in an emergency, Seeing one boy picking up stones and placing them in piles and another sitting on a fence it didn't take a crystal ball to know that it was Jack on the fence.

I could go on -- the accurate boy: If his answer differed from the one in the back of the book, the book was wrong. The girl who chased the boys with a snake, the fourth grader who liked best to read eighth grade material; but probably this is enough to make my point. In rural schools there was variety, perhaps because it was permitted.

Chapter 13
The Curriculum

Not all the learning that went on in those one-room rural schools came from books. Every meeting of minds is an adventure. Each personality is new ground and leads to fresh viewpoints, enlightening and enriching. If two children think exactly alike, one of them isn't thinking. If what they write is exactly alike, one has probably copied. If a poor speller sets down a long, correctly spelled word you know he copied.

In the study of English the diagram for purpose of analysis that had once been the backbone of grammar had gone out and was slowly creeping back in. In 1916-17 it was optional.

For some pupils it clarified sentence structure. For others it was a useless burden. Those who used the English language most competently came from homes where it was correctly spoken.

We were in an era of flash cards -- in arithmetic for beginners to recognize figures, for older ones to add, subtract and multiply. Flash cards were to the teacher what a thermometer is to a nurse. She was seldom seen without one -correction, without a handful of them.

The study of geography had turned from map study to the consideration of people and industries. There was emphasis on one's own state (New York in our case), on the home county and township. During my years of teaching, it was combined with History and Civics to become Social Studies dealing with the progress of mankind.

Physical Training was our only compulsory frill and we largely disregarded it between the visits of the instructor. We had no music except incidentally at Christmas and small programs for special days.

The only art was an effort on the part of the children to break up the monotony of the gray walls. For this they traced and colored in their spare time. Some preferred to take their masterpieces home.

It was a time of change. By the time I finished teaching I was having classes in art and asking people with musical talent to come in at times and assist. There were no batons -I had never heard the term -- no marching except at the monthly visit of the instructor, no organized sports.

Children played whatever they pleased. It didn't have to be a game. They might choose a walk in the woods or wading in the creek.

Later on, regional Field Days were organized where schools competed against each other in running, jumping and other events, and in baseball. Some children liked these contests, others declined to take part.

Nature Study was in the curriculum but it was not stressed. Country children were fairly well versed in it anyhow. It was intended to sharpen the awareness and enrich the cultural appreciation. I treated it incidentally.

We collected pictures, old birds' nests and made charts. A little later we got into health habits. Every school was required to have its Health Club with elected inspectors who made sure that each child had cleaned his nails and brushed his teeth, and to ask if he had taken his weekly bath. One boy responded to that question,

"What?! In the wintertime? I'd freeze to death!"

Usually some minor honor or privilege was given to those who passed the cleanliness test at the top of the list and there were those who won no laurels.

One child of parents who were on public assistance is a case in point. The officer who handled his case said of him,

"His parents say he is five years old but I doubt it. I don't think he could possibly collect that much dirt in only five years."

This was intended as a witticism but in cold fact he could collect a great deal of it over a weekend. He enjoyed making a big suds at school. It was what he did best. By Friday night his hands were unnaturally white. Each Monday morning he was ready for the Lava soap and wash basin.

Emphasis was shifting from oral to silent reading with tests in comprehension to make sure the reading was understood and questions which required original thought on it. Certificates were awarded to those who read 25, 50 or 100 approved books during the school year.

The reading matter in general had a moral tone. In contrast to today's fantasy, it bristled with tales of heroism, of accomplishment in the face of odds, with poems, quotes from the Bible and from literary masterpieces.

This was true on Gobblers' Knob but again it was a time of change. By the time I finished my career much lighter reading matter was being offered. It was more realistic and reflected the changing times but not calculated to develop character. It did encourage ambition in making one's way in the world.

Perhaps some of the credit for the good civic behavior of those who matriculated in the small schools should go to the fact that they were not exposed to the world of misbehavior. No TV, no radio, social contact mostly with neighbors and relatives who shared the family standards. If there was crime in the world these children knew little of it. What little they heard seemed about as unreal as the story of the three bears and nothing that could possibly happen to them.

A great deal depended on the teacher. One who had musical talent organized rhythm bands and trained her charges to sing acceptably; a student of nature had her gray walls covered with nature lore, charts showing the arrival of spring birds, collections and pictures of birds and insects.

All teachers tried to do a minimum of all these special activities but a visitor could tell at a glance where the teacher's interest lay. It was well that teachers changed schools from time to time to give the pupils a well-rounded foundation.

Although some of these frills may seem meager since it represented all the schooling most of these children would ever have, there is something to be said for it.

Scholastically, basics were well learned from repetition and from hearing them gone over by other grades. Eight grades in a room was possible. Practical topics like money, measurements and time appealed to all. Keeping a record of time worked and computing wages were eagerly practiced. Even below average minds understood their value.

Socially all ages mingled with reasonable harmony assisted by the teacher if necessary. The group was small and teacher and children knew each other in depth.

It was customary for the teacher if she was new to the school to be invited to stay overnight in each home at least once during the school year. This was likely to occur early in the term while the unheated spare room with its crisply ironed cotton sheets would not be too uncomfortably cold.

These spare rooms were equipped with a variety of handmade art work, crocheted pillow shams (covers that protected the hand embroidered pillowcases), and were carefully removed before the bed was turned down for occupancy. The quilts were handmade, quilted in beautifully fine stitches, often made by Grandma, or even Great Grandma, and reserved for special occasions. There was often a hand crocheted spread for the bed and a matching dresser scarf, and a crocheted lambrequin embellished the clock shelf if there was one. The china bowl and pitcher set matched the chamber pot and cover -- the cover further adorned with a crocheted cover. One's last view before sleep took over was of a framed ancestor.

The living room was likely to contain potted plants, some of them in bloom. Now and then there were samplers worked in cross stitch with flowers and mottoes. And hair wreaths! One side of the wreath was made with hair from the father's side of the family, the other with hair made from the mother and her ancestors and close relatives, the top containing hair from the children of the union.

Less affluent families made do with bouquets of wild flowers, tied quilts and ancestors.

These visits helped tremendously in understanding, and indirectly in discipline and gave a sense of solidarity to the whole environment. The teacher learned the family objectives and standards, parents learned the aims of the teacher, and children got the idea that teacher and parents were in cahoots and he could not safely play the one against the other. If some of today's ills stem from lack of communication, give the one room school a credit mark.

Two unplanned minuses not confined to rural schools rose to plague everyone concerned. Epidemics of head lice and of itch were hard to combat. Until every child was clean no one was safe from contamination.

The swiftest cure for head lice was kerosene but getting rid of the smell made the cure almost as bad as the disease. It took many shampoos and the scalp became red and tender in the process.

Whatever caused the itch, it seemed to be in the books in the school library. Every time a new pupil entered school and used books from the library he developed a case of itch. This happened in one school only.

The handling of wrongdoing in the neighborhood was handled locally. Things like cheating, unauthorized pregnancies and petty theft were kept hush-hush as long as possible and the guilty parties were semi-ostracized. No one had dealings with a crook without his eyes open, and wrong-doers were very slowly admitted into the society of honest folk, never completely so. By the time neighbors had forgotten, the guilty one had formed limited friendships and seldom ventured beyond them.

A woman who used to be hired for house cleaning or when a mother was ill was recommended thus, "She isn't married and she has this child but she is a good worker. From there on let the buyer beware. We always called her Mrs. N ---."

Chapter 14
The Year of the Influenza

In the fall of 1918 my brother Donald and I had an apartment on the second floor of the Culver home. Several purposes were being served by this arrangement -- Donald would be one of my pupils, I would be "spending it where I made it" which was considered highly commendable and Donald would help me carry supplies. Mrs. Culver had been a schoolmate of mine and I felt that we were happily situated.

My reason for applying for a school so far from home was that Leon was becoming too amorous for comfort. I had been able to say no convincingly so far but the signs were right for putting distance between him and me. I was now all of fifteen miles distant -- too far in those horse and buggy days for a casual call.

The carrying chore was the weak spot. Our mother who was teaching in an adjoining district kept the other children with her at her rooming place during the school week. On Friday afternoon they would go home and she would prepare food, enough to leave at home, for them to use during the week and for Donald and me. They also brought other supplies. We did not expect to see a store during the school year.

Sunday afternoons she returned, and Sunday afternoons Donald and I walked the three miles and carried back our allotment.

On a pleasant day in the fall this was a nice

diversion. We started early, paused along the way to chat with people we knew, threw pebbles at a convenient mark, watched the birds and squirrels, or collected brilliant leaves that drifted across our path.

On the return trip we assumed the roles of pack mules as we carried such items as flour, potatoes, apples, butter, milk, vegetables and kerosene for the lamp and oilstove, along with bread and maybe cookies. We were ever mindful that kerosene and foodstuffs are not compatible.

There was likely to be more than we could carry all at once so we used the old method of carrying and setting the load down, going back for what we had set down before, thus covering the distance three times, four if we count the walk over in the first place. There was no hurry at all and we enjoyed the walk until January.

Then the load of kerosene doubled and the weather worsened. One stormy Sunday I was carrying a 25 pound flour sack with potatoes in the bottom and a smaller sack of flour on top of them. What with carrying them over my shoulder, setting the bag down in a snowy place and picking it up many times, the bag sprung a leak allowing the flour to sift down among the potatoes. When I discovered what was happening I carried it more carefully but it still seemed doubtful whether there would be much usable flour when we arrived.

We had a small conference and decided to borrow a sled.

The question arises -- why didn't we bring a sled from home? We certainly had several. I do not have the answer. Maybe we were just plain stupid.

Life in the apartment was pleasant, that is, unless communication is essential for pleasure. I was deep in trying to write poetry and Donald was inventing a differential gear not at all disturbed by the fact that there was one already in use. Our conversations ran something like this,

Donald: (thrusting a diagram between me and my

poem) Look, do you think this would work?

Me: (who hadn't the vaguest idea what he was talking about) I guess so. How does this sound--

In the church the children sing
While the bells up in the steeple ring?

Donald: All right, I guess. See, this rod connects -and so on and on.

We were sometimes diverted by the Culver children who came up for a romp with Donald or a story with me.

It was the year of the Armistice and we heard the church bells and the horns from the nearest towns and villages. It was not entirely unexpected. We had heard rumors but didn't go so far as to expect such an event.

There was a small party that evening at a neighbor's home in celebration. None present had a personal interest in the war or its end but it offered an excuse for a party.

In mid-December we went with the Culvers on a shopping trip. The town was some distance away and we went in a horse drawn sleigh. On the way home we were made aware of something we had known in a detached way all along. Mr. Culver was a drinking man. The Prohibition Amendment was very much in the news at the time and he had laid in a supply of the oh-be-joyful while in town, some of it under his belt. We laughed at his fumbling wit which he thought was hilarious and things were going quite well until he became thirsty.

He stopped the team and pulled a bottle from under the seat of the sleigh. He pointed out a small shrub in a snowy field beside the road.

"I'm going to take a drink," he announced. "Now, would any of you think any more of me if I went behind that bush to do it?"

We admitted that the scrawny little bush would make very little difference and he regaled himself generously.

One morning Donald and I heard a crash below

stairs and the door at the bottom resisted our efforts to open it. "It's no use," came Mr. Culver's voice. "The plaster has come down."

"How are we going to get to school?" There was no other exit and I was mindful of children arriving at a locked schoolhouse.

"You'll have to wait 'til we clear it away."

The ceiling plaster had fallen in one huge sheet and hung over their bed like a canopy.

One peculiarity of Mr. Culver -- when sober he was energetic and somewhat aggressive but when drunk he became quite obedient. When his wife said, "Now you shut up," he shut up.

Weeks slipped by and with spring came an opportunity to ride to town with a neighbor girl who had a pony. She had had it all winter but her parents didn't trust the combination on slippery roads. It was a pleasure to get our kerosene locally.

It was also the year of the Spanish influenza. A few people in my district had had mild attacks that they thought might be the flu but nothing serious had occurred until we heard that a family in Mother's district had been stricken with devastating suddenness. The grandfather, the father and the oldest son had succumbed within a week.

Donald and I were shaken. The son had been one of Mother's pupils and we had visited in the home. It was unbelievable. Other stories trickled in. Doctors were working day and night and could not keep up with the calls. Undertakers were similarly overworked.

Sunday was a balmy day and Donald took his bicycle on our routine trip. He pushed it up the hills and coasted down the other side where he rode in circles and figure eights until I caught up with him.

It was about four o'clock when we reached Mother's rooming place. We were told that someone had phoned. She had the influenza. At last the seriousness of the epidemic hit us at gut level. It had struck our family and all we could think of was getting home to them. I phoned my trustee that there would be no school that week and we started. The distance was eight miles.

When we reached Woodhull we heard that Mother had developed pneumonia along with the influenza. It was dark when we reached our own neighborhood and were told that she was not expected to live.

As usual these reports were exaggerated. Mother had had a bout with influenza, had been on the verge of pneumonia but was able to call from her bed when she heard our voices.

"What did you come home for? Now you are exposed." It seems that the one bright spot through her illness had been the thought that Donald and I were not exposed and might escape. It had been her ace in the hole and we had blown it.

The younger children had the flu and there was plenty of work for Donald and me to do. My father with his usual immunity to germs was acting as nurse, cook and chore-boy.

Two of the children had the croup. Dad was glad to see us. Neither of us became ill and we were all soon back in our respective places.

It had been a memorable year -- the Armistice, the influenza, Prohibition. Donald and I had each done a bit of growing up.

Chapter 15
Away From Home

The time came when I went away from home to teach-- far enough away so that my name didn't mean a thing and I must stand or fall on my own performance. It was an odd feeling. I had not been conscious of it before but the family name if it is a good one is a resource.

The cause of the move was Leon. He had become too amorous for comfort. He said he could find girls more receptive to his desires and it seemed like an auspicious time for me to leave the scene.

I was already under contract when I made the decision. It was a school my mother had taught and the trustee said he didn't care "two cent's worth" who showed up to teach. She agreed to fulfill the contract if I could find a school elsewhere.

I wrote several District Superintendents to ask if there were vacancies in their areas. The school where I located was the incredible distance of thirty-five miles from home, too far for a well-groomed horse and polished buggy.

The first person I met in the new location was the trustee, George. He came out of his large white house as my father and I drove into the yard and got out of the family Ford.

He was a tall gaunt man, slightly round shouldered. There was a hitch to his gait as he came to meet us. He carried his cap in his hand revealing a bald head fringed with sparse white hair. A small white mustache bisected his weathered face which had a ruddy cast that proclaimed that he had once been a redhead.

He told us that he had been elected trustee because the State and the Superintendent were insisting on the installation of inside, sanitary toilets in all schools and he was the only one in the district mean enough to defy the order.

No one wanted the toilets, he said, but no one else cared to face the superintendent who was, to use his own term, progressive, but in George's opinion a "ring-tailed snorter."

This was indirectly the reason George had not hired a teacher. The only applicants he had had were recommended by the superintendent. I was not. The superintendent had stressed the fact that he couldn't recommend me because he didn't know me. George wanted a teacher that would be on his side. He hired me at once.

The next hurdle -- where would I stay? I preferred to room. George thought this inadvisable. He reasoned that my path would be smoother if someone in the district was getting a share of my money, and implied that the going would be rough at best with him as trustee.

"You can stay with us for a week or two until you can find a place," he offered.

This gave my father an idea. "You've got a big house. Why can't she room here?"

George wriggled gleefully back and forth inside his shirt to indicate that it was an interesting question and shook his head. He followed us to the car and explained,

"My housekeeper is hard to get along with. It would never work."

"Genieva can get along with anyone," my father assured him. Possibly "put up with anyone" would have been more accurate. It was agreed that I would stay with them while making arrangements.

George's house had been a stage stopover in days gone by. It had five bedrooms and a large hall upstairs.

I was charmed with his housekeeper, Molly. She had a rugged Irish face that broke into a nice smile. She treated me rather formally, "Would ye come to yer dinner, Miss?" and "Thank 'e, Miss," when I stacked my dishes at the close of the meal.

Arrangements proved difficult. He was correct about his unpopularity and its effect on me. The neighbors tended to look upon "George's teacher" as the last and least in excellence. One woman offered to board me but he vetoed it on the grounds that she lived just over the imaginary line in another district and besides, she was not very well liked.

He guessed that people were torn between curiosity on the one hand and fear for their reputations on the other. A second offer I was advised to refuse because Mrs. Johns was such a gossip that my every move would be broadcast and discussed. This did not concern me. I felt that my moves would be above reproach. As it turned out, my moves, though innocent enough, would have caused much grist for Mrs. John's mill.

There was an empty cheese factory in the district and I proposed living in it. This was disapproved by all as there would be no chaperone. This was a new idea to me. I had always taken full responsibility for my behavior. I wondered what kind of young men lived in George's district.

In the end George weakened and let me have a room over his living room and I settled in knowing that I would be tarred with his brush if I wasn't already. I think he decided he would rather have firsthand knowledge of my doings than hear of them from the neighbors.

He not only rented me the room for practically nothing, he set up a stove for me, furnished me with wood at a nominal price, gave me milk and vegetables, and sometimes transported me to teachers' conferences which was the only place I went farther than I could walk.

Next I met the family across the road. There was a young man, Tom Grant, and it was only a matter of time

With a Capital O

until he and his fifteen-year-old sister, Betsey, asked me to attend a party in their company. I was eager to go though George warned that the Grants did not move in the highest circles.

It was an interesting evening. We had barely started when group of young men pelted us with green apples. We escaped the fusillade by virtue of the speed of Tom's nag. He wasn't fast but, encouraged by the whip, managed to out distance boys on foot. I was sharply critical of those young men. There was a similar group at home which I called the "Donkey Club." Tom and Betsey defended them especially on K.P. who, they declared, was a nice person.

The party was a further revelation. They were still in the kissing game era and there was not a trace of tobacco smoke all evening. Some of the games were active to the point of roughness. It seemed to me that the clocks had been turned back a dozen years.

There were singing games with which I was familiar and I noticed that an older man led the singing and kept things moving. I was surprised that a leader was provided. Later I learned that he also served as chaperone without which no party would have been permitted.

George was convinced that the neighbors would pump me for information about him which they did and that they would move heaven and earth to get a look into my room which he forbade. He made it a condition of my staying that I did not discuss his affairs, good or bad.

His shortcomings were revealed to me bit by bit as I grew better acquainted. The first and most glaring was Molly with whom, they persisted, he was living in sin. It was obvious to me that this was not true but my lips were sealed. Molly had a stout lock on her bedroom door which was on the second floor not far from my room while George slept downstairs. Her favorite motto was "Death before dishonor," and she told me that she had insisted on the lock before she spent a night in the house.

In the classroom there was calm and I was invited to spend a night with first one, then another family until I had made the rounds. In each case George gave me a rundown on the family and they gave me a few pointers about George.

To get groceries I walked two and a half miles to a small grocery store unless George happened to be going to a larger town. It became the custom for Betsey and I and any small fry who might attach themselves to us to make the trip on a Saturday afternoon. We took along a baby carriage that had been converted to a grocery cart by Tom. It was called Solomon John from the character in Peterkin Papers.

As time went on various other people including the teacher in the adjoining district joined the group and there was a great deal of chatter, laughing and singing -- enough to attract unfavorable comment.

Once we were scattered by a cow, one of a herd a woman was driving to pasture. The woman scolded us for being scared by a perfectly well behaved cow.

Other interesting distractions came up. One Saturday I saw a large stone tipped on its edge in a field beside the road and quoted the old superstition that restoring such a stone to a horizontal position was an occasion for making a wish. This was an opportunity none of us wanted to miss and we climbed down over the bank and undertook to tip the stone. It was large and heavy and embedded for half its bulk in hard sand. We could not budge it.

The more it resisted our efforts the more determined we became. Tree branches used as levers helped not at all.

Meanwhile Solomon John sat beside the road loaded with groceries. A man came along, stopped his team and peered over the bank. The fact that he was an eligible bachelor was not lost on us.

"What are you trying to do?" he asked.

We explained enthusiastically.

"Well, if that stone's got to be turned, I'll have to

help," he said. "You'd better get those groceries home before a hungry dog comes along," and he joined us leaving team and wagon beside the road with Solomon John.

So much for Saturday afternoons. Tongues wagged. And Saturday afternoons were only a beginning.

Chapter 16
Behind the Scenes

The adult population of George's district seemed (to me) to feel that anything they could not inspect must be bad, Perhaps they were only curious, and peeved because they might be missing something. On the other hand, this is a rather common view of young people. Maybe we were prejudiced.

Saturday afternoon activities paled beside those carried on under cover of darkness. Every Sunday night resembled Hallowe'en. Couples who started out for a ride or to go to church were likely to be stopped, their horses unhitched and led away, Heaven only knew where, the harness taken apart and hung in someone's barn. Buggy wheels were changed. As to who was riding with whom, it was all a hopeless scramble.

Pedestrian church goers sometimes lent a hand.

A party at the schoolhouse was broken up by boys who said they were not invited. This was perfectly ridiculous as such affairs were always open to all. They stuffed cabbages into the chimney and smoked the guests out. After that they opened the chimney and affably joined the party.

There were many similar incidents. It was a carefree, robust time and place, at least in playtime.

There were exceptions to the casual friendliness. George had been quite right about Molly. I found her difficult at times. She had been widowed in Ireland at a young age, had been a domestic servant in England and in

With a Capital O

Canada, finally coming to the United States in that capacity. She considered her position with George in that light.

She refused to join in neighborhood festivities on the grounds that a servant does not belong in her master's social circle, and must never take anything from his household. George urged her to attend the picnic for the last day of school but she was adamant in her refusal.

It was years later after she married George that I learned her reason. The marriage made a great difference to Molly. She was fond of saying, "Now that I am mistress of the house --" This mystified George who didn't see any social difference.

In the meantime she had an irritating habit of drawing into herself for a week or more at a time. During these intervals she performed her duties meticulously wearing a frown an inch thick and not opening her mouth to speak so much as a word. My "Good morning" fell into a pool of heavy silence.

I was a person who liked to be liked and I worried lest I had done something to offend her.

"Just don't notice it. She'll get over it," George advised.

Sure enough, some morning no different from other mornings so far as I could see, she would appear all smiles and ready with her Irish wit. She was a charming person between sulks, playing George's old Edison phonograph with the enormous lily shaped horn, and dancing around the kitchen, freezing ice cream in a snowbank and making pungent comments about the neighbors whom she knew largely through George's tales.

She could give advice. The morning after I had stayed out late visiting with a fellow teacher, she told me, "She may know what's in the book, but she is ignorant in many ways, to stay out after midnight."

When I had been keeping company with people she considered undesirable, she commented, "You lie with dogs, you rise with fleas."

Years later after her promotion to mistress of the house she told me that her temperamental spells had not been personal, but she had been annoyed by something about the house.

Any puzzling questions that arose among the young people were promptly settled by Betsey's Ouija board. She said that once it had told her that she would live on the hill with K.P. In this it erred. She married a handsome man she met later while "working out".

Betsey had the bright idea that we should dig a big mess of dandelion greens in season and go up and surprise K.P. with a dandelion supper. Tom joined us and their mother sent other edibles. This was well as K.P. did not like dandelion greens.

The Donkey Club found out where we were and laid siege to the house. We turned out the lights. The aggressors threw water, pails of it, with deadly accuracy at anyone who peered out a window or door.

The defenders exhausted the supply of water in the house and were quite weaponless. This went on until nearly dawn. The living room floor of wide, bare boards was wet and we were soaked. Approaching daylight ended the party since all concerned were faced with a day's work.

I feared stern disapproval but those who knew were too deeply involved to tell. The house was three quarters of a mile from the nearest dwelling and no one heard the commotion. That was one sin I did not have to answer for.

This sort of thing worried George. He was desperately anxious for his teacher to be accepted and approved, and for his term of office to be a success. He pitted himself against the gossips who would have liked to have him fail. I suppose they did their best but the results were not much of a problem. Their children were likely to be heavily involved in whatever I was doing. The worst I ever heard about myself was that a passerby had seen my wash on the line and had noted patches. All felt that anyone earning the munificent salary they were paying me could afford something better.

George was something of a psychologist and he knew the community like he knew the palm of his roughened hand. He was usually able to get me out of any difficulty.

One Monday morning when I arrived at the schoolhouse the flag pole was missing. Everyone Ooh'd and Ahh'd and wondered. There was no getting a confession out of any of the pupils, though I was sure that some of them knew quite well where it was and how it got there. I didn't try. I reported it to George.

He mulled the matter over and came to a decision.

"I'm sure Oscar was into it. That boy is a ring leader. If he didn't do it, he knows who did. If he didn't know at the time, he does now. I'll fix it."

So, after supper, he hitched up old Major and drove down the road. It was about chore time and he managed to see Oscar's father and stop to chat. In the course of the conversation, Mr D-- asked how school was going. This was a stock question. Practically everyone asked it. School loomed large in their lives.

George shook his head sadly. "I'm afraid the boys have gone too far this time," he said.

"Why?" Mr. D-- was all ears.

"They took the flag pole. That's school property, you know. We know who did it. I'm going to set the troopers on them if it ain't back in the morning."

They exchanged comments on the crops and the weather, and George drove on.

The flag pole was back in place the next morning. No comments from anyone.

Chapter 17
Decorum

It seems that my deportment which I had thought would be exemplary did not meet local standards.

Being far from home, I was usually standing beside the mailbox when the carrier stopped on Saturday, the only day I was free to do so. I wrote voluminous letters home to my family who answered only when something important occurred, like my brother's appendectomy, my sister's engagement and when the best cow died.

The carrier was a friendly man in his thirties or forties. I never gave a thought to his age or marital status. He had an eye for the women and flattered me ridiculously.

One Saturday he said, "How would you like to ride around the route with me?"

"How would I get back?"

"I'd bring you back."

"Oh, I'd like it."

He was an entertaining companion and pointed out places of interest along the way: the buckwheat mill said to be the largest in the world, the farm with the highest assessed valuation in the township, the home of a man who had recently made the headlines by committing suicide.

When we reached the town where the post office was located, he stopped in front of the only hotel.

"I'd love to take you home to dinner," he said. "But my wife has a jealous disposition. You have dinner here. I'll come back soon and take you over the rest of the route and home."

I was perturbed to hear of his wife, and to have him pay for my dinner but there didn't seem to be anything I could do about it at the moment so I enjoyed my meal.

He took me back as promised stopping at my schoolhouse to peek in the back window to "see where the little girl works."

I made a mental note not to ride with him again. Fine. But when the account of my ride went the rounds, I heard plenty. Most of the good ladies would not collect their mail until he was out of sight because of his unwelcome attentions. The minister's wife had tried to convert him by reading tracts to him when he stopped at their box but had given up when he persisted in calling her sweetheart.

They all pronounced him a terrible character with whom no decent woman would be caught dead. I learned later that he was a scoutmaster in his home town and well respected.

There were other straws in the wind. I walked to the crossroads church to attend an evening evangelical meeting and the evangelist brought me home. I went as one of a group to a more distant church to a revival meeting. We went in a surrey -- an old couple, several children, the evangelist and I. We picked up an extra for the return trip and I rode home on his lap. After that, a nice old lady invited me to spend revival nights at her home, sleep on the couch in her front room and walk home decently by daylight.

One teacher in the area was threatened with having her contract cancelled. The hussy bobbed her hair and wore a sleeveless dress. To school, no less. I escaped those errors, but I did have a blouse that was thought to be cut too low in the neck. The minister's wife helped me sew lace around the neckline. Bit by bit I learned the facts of life in George's school district.

By this time I had become acquainted with K.P.'s family, had been a guest in the home, received the stamp of their approval, and had gone out with him a few times.

The family consisted, besides K.P. and his parents, of a school teacher sister of sound reputation and an older spinster sister, also blameless. There was a married sister and a married brother also of spotless records.

It was not long before their approval, plus their spotless reputations began to have a salutary effect on my doubtful one. I was being referred to occasionally as K.P.'s girl rather than scoffingly as George's teacher, a small but significant advancement.

Chapter 18
Discipline

A friend of ours who had once taught school was fond of commenting on the experience thus, "I trod the hurricane deck of a schoolroom for three years." I don't know exactly what he had in mind but when I think of the term he used, I think of discipline.

Ideally, discipline is a by-product, not a struggle. I wish I could say it was always so with me, but there were times--

One school year's discipline was thrown out of balance by putting off 'till tomorrow what should have been done today, and by a family of mice.

I had been out of the schoolroom for several years and had acquired a husband and three children along with other responsibilities. Curricula change from time to time, and I planned to rely heavily on the State syllabus for guidance. Instead of checking ahead of time, I opened the desk drawer on opening day to a family of mice and a pile of chewed up paper barely recognizable as the State syllabus. The District Superintendent ordered a new one for me but it was slow in coming.

In the meantime we had to start somewhere, a little like "flying by the seat of your pants," I suppose. But I was not able to recover from the blow dealt me by those mice. With me, discipline hinges on scholarship, and we were a long time getting on the right track.

It was in George's school that I made the acquaintance of the pungent leek. I shattered tradition by permitting the children to eat them, worse yet by eating them myself. People now travel long distances to attend leek dinners, but it was not so in George's district at that time. I had never seen, smelled or heard of them when one of the children asked if I would let them eat leeks. I said, "I don't care what you eat. What are leeks?"

That question was soon answered. The children went to the woods, and leeks were soon coming in by the armful. I was offered some and, like Adam, I did eat. A few of the more fastidious pupils averted their faces and held their noses when one of the polluted ones came near. I should have been warned. I found them delicious.

Mrs. Johns came over to George's that evening to set me straight on the subject of leeks. It seems that she could detect the odor of leeks on the breath for a week. She spoke in glowing terms of teachers past who had walloped anyone daring to show up in school with a trace of leeks on his breath. I had done the unforgivable, and she looked forward to the battle that would follow at school.

There was nothing I could do about the leeks we had already consumed. The Johns family would have to suffer through the week but, from that day forward, we gathered leeks, each one making his own individual pile and eating nary a one until, on Friday night, we took them home. At least those who dared to do so took them home. It was then up to the parents to wallop if they so desired.

I gave myself a good mark for getting results with a word rather than a walloping but I had an uneasy feeling that Mrs. Johns would not agree.

I enjoyed my leeks on Friday night for supper (farmers' supper, the evening meal). Later that evening someone got up a party. This was not unusual. Parties spawned at the drop of a word. I went, of course. I brushed my teeth and tried to keep my mouth closed when near others. All went well until about eleven o'clock when warm sugar was being served. One of the most attractive young men gave his sister an accusing look and said, "Who's been eating leeks?"

It was an embarrassing moment when I confessed.

There was also the snowball fight. It was the stormiest interval of my teaching career.

The time had come when the children were overdoing the throwing of hard packed snowballs, sometimes either by accident or design, hitting smaller children. The conventional lecture proved ineffective. One thing led to another until I found myself standing (challenging) the entire school.

I was enraged at their apparent cowardice. I think I was trying to demonstrate that one does not shrink from heavy odds and attack helpless victims. I was beyond speech, somewhat in the position of a man who stood his neighbor on his head and jiggled him up and down.

"You can't tell the darn fool anything," he explained, "I thought I'd show him something."

I was very thoroughly snowballed and scored a few direct hits myself. One of the older boys called it off before time to ring the bell.

I was acutely ashamed of my performance. It was not the dignified, scholarly way. Not much better than walloping. I envisioned what Mrs. Johns would say about it.

To my surprise I did not hear any comments from her. I gathered that the children had not mentioned it at home. Perhaps they were as ashamed as I.

I still can't understand why it should have brought anything except disaster down on my head but, strangely, the problem faded out.

By this time K.P. and I were going steady, and I was less concerned about neighborhood gossip.

Chapter 19
Board – Again

On Kalb Hill the subject of board nearly cost me my job. The trustee, Edt Braun, was a German-American as was nearly everyone in that district. I loved their accent, the soft g's and sh sounds and the trace of a d before a t, or vice Versa. They referred to themselves as "barnyardt Tdutch."

Edt was gray haired, heavily built and, on the night I applied for the school, seemed expansively genial. He introduced his heavy set, smiling wife and his four children-- Etna (Edna), Rosse (Rose), Edt and Pill (Bill). They smiled shyly and were silent.

Mr. Braun's face creased in proud complacency.

"Goot poys," he said with a fond gesture toward the children who stood in a row like so many tin soldiers. The amenities being disposed of, he laid down some rules for the conduct of the school.

"I tdon't vant no nonsense apout keeping them kits after school. I tdon't like to see them come straggling home, vun or two at a time like they hate vun another. Ven they come they all come, If they tdon't get their lessons, lick 'em."

"Und none of this hot lunch pissness. My kits got goot stummicks. They eat vat's in the pail. Other kits the same. They're Dtutch. They tdon't need coddling. Treat 'em rough if you vant to, put tdon't coddle 'em."

We signed a contract and he told me that the woman who usually boarded the teacher was ill but that Gert Gross would board me.

I stopped to see Mrs. Gross and was absolutely

scandalized at the price she was asking. At once the spectre of the mortgage rose before my eyes and I refused her offer.

The schoolhouse was about three miles from George's place and I occupied my old quarters there for a few days until I could find a less expensive place to board. I told Mr. Braun that I could not afford the price.

He disagreed. "I gif you goot money," he said. "You can afford it."

How clear is hindsight! I remembered then that he had given me more than I asked, evidently so that Gert could profit by it.

I insisted that I would not pay so much so he obligingly moved Walter Brotz and his sister, Myrtie, into an unoccupied house in the district. They would board me much cheaper, he said.

They would and I moved in. They were poor which I didn't mind. Everything was plain but clean. I didn't mind that they were ignorant and I overlooked the fact that Walter was grossly overweight and sat in what could only be described as a heap. He also sat with his mouth hanging open and, at times, he drooled. Myrtie was also overweight but slightly more shapely. I was prepared to put up with these deficiencies in the interests of thrift, or shall we say greed? It was all for the mortgage.

I spent very little on myself.

Mr. Brotz' means of getting from place to place was a scraggly old gray horse, and presently he planned to do something about that. He started negotiating for a car, secondhand, of course. He planned to make the payments with what he would receive from me.

A salesman came, eager to deal. He asked if Walter had ever driven a car. (One look had raised a doubt) Walter admitted that he had not but, he said, the school teacher would be driving it.

The salesman asked me about it and Walter expanded on the theme. He and I, he said, could go to town in the car without having Myrtie along. So, that was what he had in mind! I refused point blank, and went back to George's. Romantic attentions was the one thing I could not overlook.

Mr. Braun blew his stack. He had told me a goot place to board, he said. I wanted a cheap place and he had provided one. What did I expect? He gave me the rest of the week to get settled in the Kalb Hill district, or else. He said he had a teacher, ready, able and willing at the lift of a telephone receiver, and he reached for it suggestively. It was a good bluff. I don't know that he could have made good on it, but I was as eager as he to settle.

It was a long way from Braun's to George's. I thought if I could reach the crossroads, the minister and his wife would keep me overnight. After all, they kept any stray who happened along, and they knew me quite well. That was about four miles, and it was supper time when I left Braun's. Mrs. Braun was cooking something that smelled delicious, but that had nothing to do with me and my problem.

A thunder storm came up, and I ran along that lonely road getting wetter by the minute. At last I came to a house that seemed to be occupied, stopped and asked for shelter from the shower. The people received me graciously and, when it appeared that the rain had settled into a night's downpour, allowed me to sleep on their davenport.

I arose early and was at the door when my hostess appeared. They had been digging potatoes, and the rain meant a day of rest. There was no time for breakfast but she gave me a glass of milk.

I walked over the hills to my schoolhouse wondering how long I could call it mine. Etna Braun divided her lunch with me at noon. The children rallied around and said they hoped I would stay. The teacher Mr. Braun was about to call, they said, was old and ugly. They tdidn't vant her.

On my way to George's after school, I was passing a house and stopped to chat with a thin, sun browned woman working in her garden. I told her who I was and why I was there.

"I will board you," she offered. "I told Mrs. Braun the night of the school meeting that I would like to board the teacher."

She named a price I could afford and the crisis was over.

But another was brewing.

Chapter 20
The Schwingles

The Schwingles where I went to board, like the others of Kalb Hill, were German Americans. Mr. Schwingle was a quiet man, rather deaf, round faced and rosy cheeked. He had lost a leg in an accident and the artificial replacement squeaked every time he swung it forward to take a step.

This disability limited his activity on the farm. To drill grain he mounted the horse drawn drill, assisted by his wife, and seated himself on a homemade seat. From there he guided the team while she ran along behind to operate the levers.

They spoke English but German was their native tongue. In an emergency it was German that came out first. One day they were having difficulty with the well fed, mettlesome team. One of the horses swung its hind quarters away from its mate and toward Mr. Schwingle who pivoted on his good leg and narrowly missed falling.

Mrs. Schwingle seized the errant beast by the bridle and yanked his head to one side effectively bringing him into line. While this was going on, there was a barrage of excited German. The first English words that surfaced were emphatic oaths.

Potatoes was the chief money crop in the area and they were dug by hand. One used a potato hook, a forklike tool with curved tines mounted on a hoe handle. Hill by hill the tubers were yanked out with the hook and landed in a neat pile ready to be picked up.

With a Capital O

Some farmers had horse drawn diggers by which a huge reel scattered the potatoes over a wide space. It was faster but very inconvenient for those who picked up the potatoes and the hook was still widely used.

Mrs. Schwingle was eager to begin. "There's only twelve acres," she said. "I can dig them alone."

And she did, picked them up, loaded the filled crates on a wagon, and carried them into the cellar where she emptied them into bins.

The cuisine did not suffer while she put in long hours in the field. It was her boast that she could put a meal on the table within fifteen minutes from the time she reached the kitchen.

Such meals! Homemade bread, homemade butter. Mr Schwingle churned the cream evenings when his wife was there to wash and work the butter. Cottage cheese we had, loaded with cream, and vegetables fresh from the garden.

The secret was planning. Potatoes were sliced ready to fry, done while the horses ate at noon. Mr. Schwingle took care to have a fire in the range when she drove in with the load of potatoes.

I was young, nimble and farm bred, but very little help she would accept from me. She prepared everything so far ahead that when I offered she was likely to say, "Ach, I have it a'ready."

In winter one of her favorite dishes was vegetable soup- a large kettle of it containing an assortment of vegetables and a bay leaf from the tree in the corner brought from Germany by her grandmother. At the last minute she would drop in a chunk of butter the size of an egg and a cup of sweet cream. If any of it remained at the close of the meal, she asked which one of us was ailing.

Such lunches as she packed for me to take to school! Beef sandwiches, homemade doughnuts, pudding or pie -- well, I had my first overweight and my first upset stomach while I was boarding at Schwingles.

She partook generously of the same fare and never gained an ounce but she was on a birdlike trot from morning 'till night. If she sat down, she was piecing a quilt, crocheting, or making a garment for one of the family.

Or for me. With her help and that of her daughters when they were home, I made dresses, skirts, blouses and aprons; hemmed tablecloths, towels and pillowcases, crocheted doilies and generally made ready for my coming marriage to K.P.

Far from being a strict chaperone, she urged K.P. to come before dark and stay until broad daylight to avoid the pitfalls of darkness along the road.

At Christmas time the girls were home. A Christmas tree was set up in the unheated parlor and decorated well ahead of the day with pieces of hard candy and homemade cookies cut in fancy shapes with a knife and frosted. The tree was left standing until it began to shed its needles in February or March. Whenever anyone wanted a cookie or a piece of candy he went in and cut it off the tree. Mr. Schwingle played the Christmas tunes on his accordion and the girls and their mother sang the songs in German and in English.

The day before the younger daughter was to start back to college there was a heavy snowfall and the wind whistled ominously around their hilltop house. Mrs. Schwingle who feared no wind or weather for herself was imploring the daughter to phone her excuses and not make her father take her to the train, about five miles distant.

The girl pointed out that she would get demerits if she were late for classes and that the snow would be there for several days with no definite end in sight.

"Which would you rather, take those demerits or hear that your father had frozen to death on the way home?" her mother asked. She seemed confident that he would reach the station safely. I think she relied heavily on feminine management.

"There are houses all along the way. He could stop if he got cold."

"You know he wouldn't."

One wonders that she did not propose taking the daughter to the station herself, but she never did. Perhaps it was an unwritten law that the head of the family should be the one to venture forth in bad weather.

As a matter of cold fact the Schwingles had a son living along that road but a family disagreement would have made a call there painful. I wondered if the details of that trouble were running through their heads.

The son had become convinced that the way to make a farm pay was to use modern machinery. Under the influence of eager salesmen he had invested beyond his ability to pay. When notes fell due before the anticipated golden harvest, he had signed his father's name.

The inevitable happened. Mr. Schwingle honored the signatures. The home farm was mortgaged for the second time, and my hosts were hoping to finish payment on it from the twelve acres of potatoes and from me.

In the meantime morning dawned clear, cold and windless. Preparations were under way early. When I came down for breakfast, several chairs were heaped with extra blankets, heated soapstones and warm clothing. Hot bricks and a lighted lantern were ready to carry under the robes.

When the two had set out in a flurry of bundling and admonitions, I set out for my one mile walk to school.

In the spring the son left the area leaving no forwarding address and a sheaf of unpaid notes. His wife and year-old son came to Schwingle's to live while she looked for employment. She was Edt Braun's daughter. One wonders why she did not go to them.

She found work and, according to rumor, tried to arrange to pay the indebtedness but was told that it had gone into the courts and could not be settled without a formal trial. After an interval, she and the baby dropped quietly out of sight and knowledge of her friends on Kalb Hill.

A number of years later when her mother died, the family advertised widely by radio and newspaper asking her to come home but there was no response.

The Schwingles had a surprise birthday party for me in the spring. To satisfy herself that I suspected nothing, Mrs. Schwingle served green onions for supper. I ate my share and she was sure that the surprise was complete.

Her favorite comment comes to mind when I doubt my ability to cope.

"You can do it."

I usually could and, if failure threatened, she was ready with a capable hand.

Now to leave the Schwingles and go to the Saeurbiers.

Chapter 21
Compulsory Attendance

Presumably the Compulsory Attendance law has gained unquestioned obedience since Heinrich Saeurbier defied it in the Kalb Hill School District about 1920. It was generally accepted then. Even on Kalb Hill, with the one exception, attendance was excellent. Exactly what possessed Heinrich remains a mystery.

His son, Curtis, did not show up at school the first day. This was before the school census and I discovered his absence through a chance remark among the children.

Instead of making a mad rush for the playground when they had finished their lunches, Kalb Hill children methodically closed their pails and like miniature Dutchmen settled themselves for a visit.

"How did the heifer you got of Heinrich turn out? Did she freshen?"

"Oh, yes, a fine heifer calf she had."

"Heinrich's cutting wheat today. Maybe that's vy Curt tdidn't come to school. "

"Who is Curt?" I asked.

"Curt Saeurbier. He's the tall one. Makes Otto look small, don't he, Otto?"

"He sure duss." Otto was a head taller than I, Curt must be tall indeed.

When he failed to come the second day, I walked home with the Braun children and spoke to the trustee about it. This was the approved way to deal with a breach of the attendance law.

"It iss nothing, "Mr. Braun assured me. "If Heinrich keeps Curt at home, he hass goot reason."

"What about the law?"

"Shust you rest easy," he advised. "If he tdon't come Monday go up and talk with Heinrich. He's a goot fellow. He'll do the right thing."

"Maybe it would be better if you talked with him."

"No, no, I got wheat to cut. You go up. Heinrich iss a goot man."

So on Monday after school I went up. And I do mean up. The Saeurbiers lived at the top of a hill. To reach the house one followed a winding dirt road for a long country mile. Edna Braun went along to introduce me to Rosie (the s soft as in silly) Saeurbier, Heinrich's daughter, and to report back to her father.

Rosie opened the door. She was a nice looking girl apparently about twenty years old.

"How tdo you tdo?" she said politely. "Come in and set. The men tdidn't come in yet. They'll be soon."

Heinrich came, a giant of a man with brisk firm step and complacent unworried eyes. He was followed closely by Curt who was all of six feet six but thin and undeveloped. He did not speak but nodded pleasantly.

I explained my errand as tactfully as I could.

"I haf always used my own chudgment about sending my shildren to school, " he said matter-of-factly. "I think I always vill. I need Curt at home." He spoke with unruffled finality.

"I'll have to notify the truant officer," I said uneasily.

"I am not afraid of the truant officer."

" -- and the District Superintendent."

-- or him either."

I had a healthy respect for the law though Heinrich might not and I telephoned the superintendent. He, too, took the law seriously.

"Send a card to the truant officer," he directed me

With a Capital O

crisply. "Notify him every day that boy is absent."

Every day for the rest of the month of September a card went out to C.C. Winehart, the truant officer. He must have been a Dutchman, too, for he ignored the situation.

When the September report went in to the superintendent things began to happen. His car turned in at the schoolhouse the next afternoon. He was not entirely unexpected.

Mr. Larkin, the superintendent, was a dapper little man, very neat, very correct. He looked over the room with a critical eye. Every child was absorbed in study. When he turned to speak to me, every eye was upon him. "Is Curtis Saeurbier present?"

"No, he isn't."

"Why not?"

"I don't know."

"It's your business to know. Your report indicates that he has not been present at all since school opened."

"That's right. He hasn't."

"You realize, of course, what this means. Both you and Mr. Braun could be in serious trouble."

Privately I was sure that Mr. Larkin was in the same brand of trouble.

"Did you notify the truant officer?"

"Every day as you told me."

"Has he called?"

"Not at school."

"I'll see him," said Mr. Larkin in a tone that implied an end to the nonsense.

October was like a carbon copy of September -- no Curt, no truant officer and a card to C.C. Winehart every day. When the October report reached Mr. Larkin it brought a sharp response but no Curt.

Finally one cold dark day in November a horse drawn buggy turned in at the schoolhouse. Eddy Braun who sat near a window raised in his seat and gave a report.

"He's awful old. He's fat. I think it's the truant officer. I tdon't think he can scare Heinrich."

Eddy was right. It was the Truant Officer and he was in a foul mood. On his way to the Saeurbier home the wind hit him full force taking his breath away and blowing out the lantern which he had relighted at considerable inconvenience. He had been jounced up and down over the frozen ruts until his bones ached. He was said to have told Heinrich that anyone who lived on that God-forsaken mountain ought not to have to go anywhere.

He went back to town and resigned his position. Curt did not come to school.

When this was reported to Mr. Larkin, he came.

"Have you told your trustee?" he asked me.

"The children tell him every night. Now and then I send a note."

"Tell him again and make it strong. That boy has to be in school. Send the trustee a note every day the boy is absent and send me a card." So each day a note went to Mr. Braun and a card to Mr. Larkin.

Christmas was coming up fast. Plans were being made. Mr. Zeh would bring a tree and set it up, the Braun children would bring ornaments, the Harvery would furnish candy canes which they would take home afterward for their own tree. Every family would bring a few homemade cookies. We would have a party the last day before the holiday recess.

Those cookies, I knew, would be works of art. I had watched Mrs. Schwingel make hers. She cut them into fancy shapes with a sharp knife and frosted them in colors with designs in white or contrasting color.

The day before the party the place was buzzing with excitement. Ornaments were being fastened to the tree, tinsel and crepe paper ropes were being hung by Otto mounted on a chair to reach the nails left from previous occasions. The Braun boys and Artie Shaunburg were making a fireplace to be used in the little play we would present for the parents and any other visitors who might choose to come. Lines were being practiced.

In the midst of all this activity there was a firm not to say angry knock at the door. Everyone not doing something recognizably useful scurried to a seat. Before I could get to the door it opened and Mr. Braun stomped in, very red of face. It was immediately apparent that the color was not entirely the result of winter wind.

"I got me a letter!" he exploded. "From that Larkin, the little banty. Got another one from the gover'ment. I tell you they vasn't no love letters. They said Curt has got to be in school tomorrow, and going regular. If that ain't done the district will loose its public money, und I vill be responsible."

He paused to let that sink into our minds, then continued,

"You get no vacation. Chust the party and keep on school." He threw his mittens on the floor, tossed his cap in the direction of the recitation bench, started to sit in the proffered chair, changed his mind and leaped up as if it had been a hot griddle.

"I am madt!" he declared, his eyes flashing as he paced back and forth across the front of the room. "I nefer vas madter. I went up to Heinrich's this morning. I hadt to valk. The road vas full of snow. I vas half froze ven I got there. You know vat I found? Vy, Heinrich and Curt pehint the stove playing poker. "

"Vant to know vat Heinrich said? He said he always uses his own chudgment --" He stopped. "You know vat Heinrich said. He pulled in the pot and handed the cards to Curt. 'Your deal,' he said. Shust that -- 'your deal!'"

"I went and got me a State Trooper. I nefer vanted to see a State Trooper so pad in all my life. I sent him up to light a fire cracker under that Heinrich and pring that poy to school. If he ain't here on time tomorrow, you phone me."

And Mr. Braun stormed out, cap and mittens clutched in his big hand.

There was a stunned silence in the schoolroom. As soon as the sounds of his departure died away, there was a chorus of dismay,

"No vacation! Oh dear!"

"I wanted to go to Grandma's."

I might have added to the lament -- I had plans of my own.

To break up the tide of unhappiness I said, "I'm afraid Ed and Heinrich won't be such good friends after this." I was thinking of Ed's insistence that Heinrich was a "goot man."

"Tdon't feel pad," one of the bigger girls consoled me. "They're both Tdutch. I shouldn't wonder they'll make it up."

"Well, we'll have to get something on the tree for Curt if he's coming in the morning."

Everyone hustled around and hung another box of candy and nuts, and fixed a few makeshift gifts for Curt.

He was greeted in the spirit of Christmas when he arrived next morning as calm as any Dutchman. He did the forenoon lessons and had the grace to blush when it became apparent that there were gifts on the tree for him.

"I tdidn't bring anything," he said. "I tdidn't know in time."

Everyone assured him that they had had a hard time getting things for him for the same reason, and he would please excuse it if his gifts weren't so nice as the others were receiving.

In the afternoon he sat with his long legs across the aisle listening to our little program and joined in the refreshments afterward.

"I won't be here long," he told me apologetically as the guests were leaving. "My Dad's going to get me some working papers to make it legal."

In this Curtis reckoned without Mr. Larkin whose

signature was required. The grain was sowed and the potatoes were in the ground before Mr. Larkin appended his name.

Curt was still in school the day in late April when another knock sounded on the door.

"John!" I cried as I opened it. "Come in."

My eyes sought the scar. I knew he had survived the war, had received a few widely spaced letters which I had faithfully answered, but this was the first time since his return to the States that I had stood face to face with him.

The scar was there half covered by a lock of hair worn longer than of old.

I offered a chair but he ignored it.

"Miss Bouton, I believe?" he said very formally with his best bow. "I represent the WCTU," he went on. "May I speak to your pupils for a few minutes?"

"Yes, of course."

He introduced himself using a fictitious name and gave a short but creditable temperance lecture, thanked me and started for the door. I followed hoping for a more confidential greeting but all I got was a broad wink and the words, "Do as I say, not as I do," in an undertone.

I was pleased and surprised to find that my former hero worship and reliance on John had faded into the past. I now had a base of my own.

As for the hard feelings I had anticipated between Edt and Heinrich, I overheard a little conversation that set my mind at rest. In the spring not long before the close of school, the church at the corner of the Kalb Hill Road with the main highway held its regular ice cream social. The Kalb Hill people always attended.

In walking between two long tables set up outside for the occasion, I noticed Edt Braun and Heinrich Saeurbier sitting by side eating cake and ice cream.

I heard what they were saying as they leaned toward each other like a couple of schoolboys. They seemed utterly unaware of everyone except each other. Heinrich was speaking.

"The trouble with you, Edt, you vas too damn fast."

"No such thing, Heinrich," said Edt amiably. "You vas too damn mean."

Chapter 22
Finis/ My marriage

The Kalb Hill girls were much concerned about my approaching marriage. They knew that I had been making myself a black dress trimmed in burnt orange, and warned me earnestly against wearing it at the wedding. They quoted the old couplet,

> "Married in black,
> You'll wish yourself back."

I assured them that my mother would make me a suitable dress which she did -- white organdy with hemstitching above the hem. Just to make it practical, she also made a pink underdress with crocheted trim that I could wear with, or without the organdy,

They were also distressed that I hadn't received an engagement ring. I could see no necessity for it. I had an heirloom garnet that I cherished, and the only one K.P. gave me was the wedding band.

Soon after school closed, we went to the parsonage with K.P's sister and my brother as attendants, and we were married. This was standard procedure for the time and area.

I had known only one couple, my brother and his bride, who had a wedding, a quiet affair. As the unmarried older sister of the groom, I was "danced in the hog trough" along with an unmarried older brother of the bride. We were both thoroughly mystified never having heard of that custom.

It was misting a little the afternoon of our bridal shower. As K.P. and I took turns at the crank of the big ice cream freezer, borrowed for the occasion from a reunion, the terrible thought came to me, "What if no one at all should come, and all this ice cream?"

They came, bringing gifts, a very few of which have survived fifty-five years of use, forty-four with K.P. and eleven of widowhood.

As soon as the marriage festivities were over, we went to the house on the hill to live.

The Kalb Hill girls walked over the hill to visit us in our new home, expressed their approval and promised to come again. Just over the hill, walking distance, but our further contacts were limited to Christmas cards and an occasional note!

George and Molly were our nearest neighbors and he became our financial advisor and, from a practical point of view, our best friend. He took a fatherly interest in us and was always ready to lend money if we needed it. So very often his counsel made the loan unnecessary.

"You don't need money," he would say. "What you need is to tell (whoever was pressing us for money) --." He would then outline what we should tell him and it was usually effective. If it wasn't, George loaned.

I can see him yet breasting the blizzard winds to come to our door. He entered, strode straight through to the woodshed to assure himself that we had plenty of wood for the storm. Then he settled down for a chat before going back.

From George we learned a great deal that stood us in good stead during the Great Depression that was just around the corner.

Now that you have had this look into rural school teaching in the first two decades of the present century, answer this question -- did the girl I met beside the stream have grounds for suicide? If she was blind of heart, deaf to the music of life, and dead to the variety and richness around her, perhaps she had.

~The End~

About The Author

Genieva B. Pawling was born Genieva Bouton on March 21, 1898 in Parallel, NY and lived her entire life in western New York. She was a teacher for over 20 years while also a farm wife who raised three children. She was an accomplished poet, having many of her poems published in various magazines and books. After the death of her husband in 1966, she undertook writing books, this being the third one. She remained active even late in life, traveling domestically and internationally, as well as pursuing her interest in genealogy. Her love of poetry and literature never faded until her death in 1996 at the age of 97.